delish

— KETO FOR — DESSERT LOVERS

75+ AMAZING LOW-CARB CAKES, COOKIES & MORE!

FROM THE EDITORS OF delish

EDITORIAL DIRECTOR Joanna Saltz
FOOD DIRECTOR Lauren Miyashiro
DIRECTOR OF CONTENT OPERATIONS
Lindsey Ramsey
ART DIRECTOR Alexandra Folino
DESIGNER Christy Sabido
FOOD EDITOR Lena Abraham
ASSISTANT FOOD EDITOR Makinze Gore
TEST KITCHEN MANAGER June (Jiuxing) Xie
TEST KITCHEN ASSISTANT Justin Sullivan

Hearst Product Studio
VP, CONSUMER PRODUCTS Sheel Shah
SENIOR EDITOR Missy Steinberg
ASSOCIATE EDITOR Patricia Reyes

CHIEF CONTENT OFFICER,
HEARST MAGAZINES Kate Lewis
SVP, CHIEF REVENUE OFFICER,
HEARST DIGITAL MEDIA Todd Haskell
VP, EXECUTIVE DIRECTOR, SALES Sue Katzen

SALES DIRECTORS Corianne Carroll, Tracy Leiken Chafetz, Kimberly Parrilla
MARKETING DIRECTOR Dina Gallo
MARKETING MANAGER Nicole Guba

PUBLISHED BY HEARST COMMUNICATIONS, INC.
PRESIDENT & CHIEF EXECUTIVE OFFICER
Steven R. Swartz
CHAIRMAN William R. Hearst III
EXECUTIVE VICE CHAIRMAN Frank A. Bennack, Jr.
SECRETARY Catherine A. Bostron
TREASURER Carlton Charles

HEARST MAGAZINES DIVISION
PRESIDENT Troy Young
PRESIDENT, MARKETING
AND PUBLISHING DIRECTOR Michael Clinton
SENIOR VICE PRESIDENT,
CHIEF FINANCIAL OFFICER Debi Chirichella
PUBLISHING CONSULTANTS Gilbert C. Maurer, Mark F. Miller

Mention of specific companies, organizations, or authorities in this book does not imply endorsement by the author or publisher, nor does mention of specific companies, organizations, or authorities imply that they
endorse this book, its author, or the publisher.

Internet addresses and telephone numbers given in this book were accurate at the time it went to press.

© 2020 by Hearst Magazines, Inc.
All rights reserved. No part of this publication may be reproduced or transmitted in any form or by any means, electronic or mechanical, including photocopying, recording, or any other information storage and retrieval system, without the written permission of the publisher.

Delish is a registered trademark of Hearst Magazines, Inc.

Front Cover Photography by Emily Hlavac Green
Back Cover Photography by Andrew Bui
Interior Photography by Emily Hlavac Green, Parker Feierbach, Lucy Schaeffer, Andrew Bui, and Erik Bernstein

Library of Congress Cataloging-in-Publication Data is on file with the publisher.

978-1-950099-75-7   2 4 6 8 10 9 7 5 3 1 paperback

HEARST

IN THE WORLD OF KETO, ANYTHING IS POSSIBLE.

To be totally honest, the thought of low-carb cookie dough, birthday cake, cheesecake, ice cream, or brownies used to make us sad. We thought, *desserts without carbs couldn't be as good...right?*

Oh how wrong we were.

After extensive ingredient testing (we ❤️ you, Swerve) and experimenting in the kitchen, we discovered that there wasn't a treat that we *couldn't* make keto-friendly. Brownies? Sure. Let's throw in a peanut butter swirl (p. 62) while we're at it. Cannoli? Ditch the shells and make it a dip (p. 14). Copycat frosty? EASY (p. 136).

Our newfound appreciation for keto sweets somehow escalated into dozens and dozens of recipes too good not to share with the world. Enter: this book. Each and every pie, cupcake, or popsicle is not only a good low-carb alternative, it's a damn good dessert. And we have a feeling that even your keto-skeptic friends will agree 😉.

XO, TEAM DELISH

KETO 101

When we first began our keto journey, we looked to our keto coach (and registered dietitian-nutritionist) Lara Clevenger, MSH, RDN, CPT, for expertise and came up with three basic rules.

1 Cut down on carbs.
Limit carbs to no more than 5 percent of your total calories. For most people, that's 15 to 20 grams of net carbs per day. **Net carbs = total carbs – fiber – sugar alcohols (like erythritol, see page 5).**

2 Don't forget about protein.
Keep protein to about 15 to 30 percent of your daily calories. That's somewhere between 70 to 135 grams per day based on 1,800 calories.

3 Eat more fat.
Make sure 60 to 70 percent of your calories come from fat. Yes, it sounds like a lot, but most of this fat should be the healthy kind, like the mono-unsaturated fats in olive oil and avocados.

Now, we're adding another.

4 Treat yourself.
To Cheesecake–Swirled Brownies (page 95)! To Snickers Bars (page 58) and Funfetti Birthday Cake (page 75)! You can have all the desserts you love when you're eating keto *without* breaking the rules.

KETO-FRIENDLY BAKING INGREDIENTS WE LOVE

STEVIA

A little bit goes a long way. If using powdered stevia, look out for fillers like maltodextrin and dextrose. (This isn't something you have to worry about for liquid stevia extract.)

BLANCHED ALMOND FLOUR

We often use it as a flour replacement. When you're shopping for a bag, be sure it's blanched. Raw almond flour is very mealy in comparison when baking. If you're using almond flour, and the batter or dough seems too wet, most of the time you just need to let it rest to give the almond flour ample time to hydrate.

BUTTER

Yes, butter is carb-free. Grass-fed is preferable, according to many experts, but these recipes will work with any full-fat, unsalted sticks you've got.

CREAM CHEESE

Do we really have to explain this one? It just makes everything better.

COCONUT FLOUR

We're often asked if you can substitute coconut flour for almond flour 1:1, and the short answer is no. Coconut flour is much drier and absorbs a ton of moisture. 1 cup almond flour can be substituted by ¼ cup coconut flour.

SUGAR-FREE CHOCOLATE CHIPS

You can't have a dessert book without chocolate. We're obsessed and forever grateful for the brand Lily's. (You can find it at many grocery stores or buy it online.) Their chocolate chips are made without added sugar and are sweetened with Stevia.

SWERVE

We use the brown, granulated, and confectioners' varieties all the time. In our opinion, erythritol (the main ingredient in Swerve) is hands-down the best keto-friendly sugar. It tastes the most like real sugar and doesn't leave you with an unpleasant aftertaste.

PEANUT BUTTER

Our love for peanut butter (especially when there's chocolate involved) is extremely evident in the pages that follow. Just make sure you're using a no-sugar-added jar! And one of the creamy variety.

VANILLA EXTRACT

We've heard complaints from some keto dieters that the alcohol in vanilla extract makes it off limits. But the truth is, the amount of carbs a teaspoon here or there adds to one single serving of most recipes is negligible. If you're feeling fancy, and want to avoid any controversy, use vanilla pods.

COCONUT OIL

In this cookbook, you'll see that we mix coconut oil with melted chocolate. Doing so creates somewhat of a magic shell situation, helping the chocolate set up more quickly.

A note about sugar alcohols: Erythritol has a glycemic index value of 0. Xylitol, sorbitol, and isomalt have low GI values and are suitable on the keto diet. Maltitol, however, should be avoided.

CONTENTS

17

66

CHAPTER ONE
SWEET BITES

Double Chocolate Muffins	10
Chocolate Glazed Cake Donuts	13
Cannoli Dip	14
Cookie Dough Fat Bombs	17
Peanut Butter Fat Bombs	18
Chocolate Avocado Truffles	21
Blueberry Muffins	22
Chocolate Mug Cake	25
Caramel Turtles	26

CHAPTER THREE
POWER BARS

Berry Crumble Bars	54
Snickerdoodle Blondies	57
Snickers Bars	58
Avocado Brownies	61
Buckeye Brownies	62
Cookie Dough Bars	65
Samoa Bars	66
Key Lime Pie Bars	69

CHAPTER TWO
COOKIE SWAP

Pecan Crescents	30
Snickerdoodle Shortbread	33
Almond Thumbprints	34
Chocolate Chip Cookies	37
Walnut Snowball Cookies	38
Lemon Cookies	41
Double Chocolate Cookies	42
Magic Cookies	45
Breakfast Cookies	46
Peanut Butter Sandies	49
Copycat Oreos	50

CHAPTER FOUR
CAKES & CUPCAKES

Red Velvet Cake	72
Funfetti Birthday Cake	75
Chocolate Cake	76
Citrus-Glazed Pound Cake	79
Tiramisu Chaffle Cake	80
Sprinkles	83
PSL Cupcakes	84
Lemon Blueberry Cake	87
Perfect Buttercream	88

AMAZING CHEESECAKES

Mini Cinnamon Roll Cheesecakes	92
Cheesecake-Swirled Brownies	95
Classic Cheesecake	96
Cookies 'N' Cream Cheesecakes	99
Raspberry-Swirled Cheesecake Bars	100
Lemon Cheesecake Mousse	103

CHAPTER SEVEN

ICE CREAM, ETC.

Frozen Yogurt Bites	124
Frozen Mint Chip Pie	127
Strawberry-Lime Cheesecake Pops	128
Ice Cream Sandwiches	131
Frosty	132
Coconut Vanilla Ice Cream	135
Avocado Pops	136

PIES & COBBLERS

Pop Tarts	106
Peach Cobbler	109
Perfect Pie Crust	110
Blueberry Pie	113
Strawberry Shortcake	114
Strawberry Galette	117
Berry Crisp	118
"Apple" Crisp	121

HOLIDAY ESSENTIALS

Pumpkin Cheesecake	140
Christmas Eggnog	143
Gingerbread Cookies	144
Hot Chocolate	147
Almond Crunch Toffee	148
Pumpkin Pie	151
Best-Ever Fudge	152
Pecan Pie	155
Chocolate Mousse	156
Pumpkin Bread	159

CHAPTER ONE

SWEET BITES

DOUBLE CHOCOLATE MUFFINS

 MAKES 12   **TOTAL TIME: 25 MIN**

They look like muffins, but they kinda sorta taste like cupcakes. And we're not at all mad about that.

2 cups almond flour
¾ cup unsweetened cocoa powder
¼ cup Swerve granular
1½ teaspoons baking powder
1 teaspoon kosher salt
1 cup (2 sticks) butter, melted
3 large eggs
1 teaspoon pure vanilla extract
1 cup sugar-free dark chocolate chips

1. Preheat oven to 350° and line a 12-cup muffin pan with liners. In a large bowl, whisk together almond flour, cocoa powder, sweetener, baking powder, and salt. Add melted butter, eggs, and vanilla and stir until combined.

2. Fold in chocolate chips.

3. Divide batter among muffin liners and bake until a toothpick inserted into the middle comes out clean, 12 minutes.

NUTRITION (per serving):

280 calories
7 g protein
7 g carbohydrates
4 g fiber
1 g sugar
27 g fat
11 g saturated fat
90 mg sodium
8 g sugar alcohol

NUTRITION (per serving):

128 calories
4 g protein
26 g carbohydrates
3 g fiber
1 g sugar
12 g fat
4 g saturated fat
157 mg sodium
22 g sugar alcohol

CHOCOLATE GLAZED CAKE DONUTS

 MAKES 10   **TOTAL TIME: 1 HR**

Part of our keto journey was figuring out low-carb ways to eat all of our favorite foods. Needless to say, donuts were a top priority. If you're on Team Cake Donut, this recipe was made with you in mind.

FOR DONUTS
Cooking spray
1 cup almond flour
¼ cup Swerve granular
2 teaspoons baking powder
¼ teaspoon kosher salt
4 tablespoons melted butter
¼ cup heavy cream
2 large eggs
½ teaspoon pure vanilla extract

FOR CHOCOLATE GLAZE
1½ cups Swerve confectioners
¼ cup cocoa powder
Pinch kosher salt
½ cup water
1 teaspoon pure vanilla extract

1. Preheat oven to 350° and grease donut pan with cooking spray. (Don't forget the centers where the donut hole is!)

2. In a large bowl, whisk together almond flour, granulated sweetener, baking powder, and salt.

3. In a medium bowl, whisk together melted butter, cream, eggs, and vanilla. Fold wet ingredients into dry ingredients until just combined. Fill each donut mold ¾ full with batter.

4. Bake until donuts are golden in color and pulling away from sides of pan, 15 minutes. Let cool completely in pan before removing.

5. Meanwhile, make chocolate glaze: In a large bowl, sift together confectioners sweetener, cocoa powder, and salt. Add water and vanilla and whisk until smooth.

6. Fit a cooking rack into a medium sheet tray, then flip cooled donuts onto cooling rack. Pour glaze over donuts and let set 10 minutes before serving.

CANNOLI DIP

🍴 **SERVES 5** | 🕐 **TOTAL TIME: 15 MIN**

Frying cannoli shells is annoying as hell and not worth the carbs or effort. Plus, everyone knows the filling's the best part.

- 1 (8-ounce) block cream cheese, softened
- ¼ cup Swerve confectioners
- 2 tablespoons heavy cream
- 2 teaspoons pure vanilla extract
- ½ teaspoon orange zest (optional)
- Pinch nutmeg
- Kosher salt
- 2 ounces keto-friendly semisweet chocolate, roughly chopped

1. In a large bowl, beat together cream cheese and sweetener until smooth. Beat in heavy cream, vanilla, orange zest (if using), nutmeg, and salt.

2. Fold in chopped chocolate and transfer to serving bowl.

PRO TIP! Though we like eating this straight from the bowl with a spoon, it pairs particularly well with strawberries for dipping. (Just don't forget to factor those into your net carb count.)

14 | KETO FOR DESSERT LOVERS

NUTRITION (per serving):

237 calories
4 g protein
17 g carbohydrates
1 g fiber
2 g sugar
21 g fat
13 g saturated fat
193 mg sodium
7 g sugar alcohol

NUTRITION (per serving):

70 calories
2 g protein
2 g carbohydrates
1 g fiber
0 g sugar
7 g fat
2 g saturated fat
35 mg sodium
3 g sugar alcohol

COOKIE DOUGH FAT BOMBS

 MAKES 30 | **TOTAL TIME: 1 HR 15 MIN**

Eating one of these fat bombs feels like sneaking a giant scoop of actual cookie dough straight from the bowl. It's a glorious feeling, made even better because there's no delayed sense of guilt.

- ½ cup (1 stick) butter, softened
- ⅓ cup Swerve confectioners
- ½ teaspoon pure vanilla extract
- ½ teaspoon kosher salt
- 2 cups almond flour
- ⅔ cup sugar-free dark chocolate chips

1. In a large bowl using a hand mixer, beat butter until light and fluffy. Add sweetener, vanilla, and salt and beat until combined.

2. Slowly beat in almond flour until no dry spots remain, then fold in chocolate chips. Cover bowl with plastic wrap and place in refrigerator to firm slightly, 15 to 20 minutes.

3. Using a small cookie scoop, scoop dough into small balls. Store in resealable container in the refrigerator if planning to eat within the week or in the freezer for up to 1 month.

PEANUT BUTTER FAT BOMBS

 MAKES 16   **TOTAL TIME: 30 MIN**

Fat bombs keep you full longer, promote ketosis, and can even increase your metabolism. Store 'em in your fridge and grab a bomb anytime you feel your energy waning. Your stomach will thank you.

- 1 (8-ounce) cream cheese, softened
- ½ cup creamy sugar-free peanut butter
- ¼ cup coconut oil, plus 2 tablespoons
- ¼ teaspoon kosher salt
- ½ cup sugar-free dark chocolate chips

1. Line a small baking sheet with parchment paper. In a medium bowl, combine cream cheese, peanut butter, ¼ cup coconut oil, and salt. Using a hand mixer, beat mixture until fully combined, about 2 minutes. Place bowl in freezer to firm up slightly, 10 to 15 minutes.

2. When peanut butter mixture has hardened, use a small cookie scoop or spoon to create tablespoon-sized balls. Refrigerate 5 minutes.

3. Meanwhile, make chocolate drizzle: Combine chocolate chips and remaining 2 tablespoons coconut oil in a microwave-safe bowl and microwave in 30-second intervals until fully melted. Drizzle over peanut butter balls and place back in refrigerator to harden, 5 minutes.

4. To store, keep covered in refrigerator.

NUTRITION (per serving):

290 calories
5 g protein
5 g carbohydrates
1 g fiber
2 g sugar
28 g fat
16 g saturated fat
390 mg sodium
2 g sugar alcohol

**NUTRITION
(per serving):**

20 calories
1 g protein
2 g carbohydrates
1 g fiber
0 g sugar
2 g fat
0 g saturated fat
35 mg sodium
3 g sugar alcohol

CHOCOLATE AVOCADO TRUFFLES

 MAKES 15 | **TOTAL TIME: 30 MIN**

Avocado is extra-creamy, extremely mild in taste, and filled with good-for-you fat. It might seem weird to combine it with chocolate, but trust us, it works.

1 cup sugar-free dark chocolate chips, melted
1 medium avocado, mashed
1 teaspoon pure vanilla extract
¼ teaspoon kosher salt
¼ cup unsweetened cocoa powder

1. In a medium bowl, combine melted chocolate with avocado, vanilla, and salt. Stir together until smooth and fully combined. Place in the refrigerator to firm up slightly, 15 to 20 minutes.

2. When chocolate mixture has stiffened, use a small cookie scoop or small spoon to scoop approximately 1 tablespoon chocolate mixture. Roll chocolate in palm of your hand until round, then roll in cocoa powder. Repeat with remaining mixture.

3. To store, keep covered in refrigerator.

BLUEBERRY MUFFINS

 MAKES 12   **TOTAL TIME: 40 MIN**

If you really want to treat yourself, melt a tablespoon of butter in a skillet, halve your muffin from top to bottom, and place muffin halves cut-side down in the skillet until toasty and golden. You're welcome.

2½ cups almond flour
⅓ cup Swerve granular
1½ teaspoons baking powder
½ teaspoon baking soda
½ teaspoon kosher salt
⅓ cup melted butter
⅓ cup unsweetened almond milk
3 large eggs
1 teaspoon pure vanilla extract
⅔ cup fresh blueberries
Zest of ½ lemon (optional)

1. Preheat oven to 350° and line a 12-cup muffin pan with cupcake liners.

2. In a large bowl, whisk together almond flour, sweetener, baking powder, baking soda, and salt. Whisk in melted butter, almond milk, eggs, and vanilla until just combined.

3. Gently fold in blueberries and lemon zest (if using) until evenly distributed. Divide batter among cupcake liners and bake until tops are slightly golden and a toothpick inserted into center of a muffin comes out clean, 23 minutes. Let cool slightly before serving.

NUTRITION (per serving):

200 calories
7 g protein
13 g carbohydrates
4 g fiber
2 g sugar
18 g fat
5 g saturated fat
265 mg sodium
5 g sugar alcohol

PRO TIP!
Raspberries, strawberries, and blackberries would all be great substitutes for the blueberries. Just be sure to stay away from fruits with higher carb counts like apples, pears, or bananas.

NUTRITION (per serving):

470 calories
15 g protein
13 g carbohydrates
7 g fiber
1 g sugar
44 g fat
18 g saturated fat
530 mg sodium
33 g sugar alcohol

CHOCOLATE MUG CAKE

 SERVES 1　　 **TOTAL TIME: 5 MIN**

It's 9 p.m. on a Monday and the week is already off to a rough start. You need a warm, melty chocolate something STAT. Enter this ridiculously fast and foolproof cake. It's perhaps the easiest thing you can do to convince yourself that everything will be okay.

---

2 tablespoons butter
¼ cup almond flour
2 tablespoons cocoa powder
1 large egg, beaten
2 tablespoons sugar-free chocolate chips
2 tablespoons Swerve granular
½ teaspoon baking powder
Pinch kosher salt
¼ cup whipped cream, for serving

1. Place butter in a microwave-safe mug and heat until melted, 30 seconds.

2. Add remaining ingredients except whipped cream and stir until fully combined. Microwave for 45 seconds to 1 minute, or until cake is set but still fudgy.

3. Top with whipped cream before serving.

CARAMEL TURTLES

MAKES 10 | **TOTAL TIME: 1 HR 5 MIN**

If you need a sweet pick-me-up (or know a friend who does), make these. You can't look at these caramel turtles and *not* smile.

FOR CARAMEL
2 tablespoons butter
⅓ cup Allulose sweetener
¼ cup heavy cream
½ teaspoon pure vanilla extract
Pinch kosher salt

FOR TURTLES
½ cup sugar-free chocolate chips, melted
50 toasted pecan halves
Flaky sea salt

1. In a small saucepan over medium-low heat, melt butter. When butter has melted and foam has subsided, stir in sweetener, cream, vanilla, and salt.

2. Bring mixture to a low simmer and cook, untouched, for 15 minutes. Transfer mixture to a medium heat-proof bowl and let cool 30 minutes.

3. Line a small baking sheet with parchment paper, then arrange pecan halves into 10 stars. Spoon about 2 teaspoons caramel into center of each star, then refrigerate to harden slightly, 10 minutes.

4. In a microwave-safe bowl, place chocolate chips and microwave in 30-second intervals until fully melted. Top turtles with a spoonful of chocolate and a sprinkle of flaky sea salt. Refrigerate until caramel and chocolate are set, about 30 minutes.

PRO TIP!
Allulose is a natural sugar found in wheat, figs, and raisins. It's not a sugar alcohol (like erythritol), and it does not cause a spike in glucose.

**NUTRITION
(per serving):**

151 calories

2 g protein

16 g carbohydrates

3 g fiber

0.47 g sugar

13 g fat

6 g saturated fat

205 mg sodium

6 g sugar alcohol

SWEET BITES | 27

CHAPTER TWO

COOKIE SWAP

PECAN CRESCENTS

 MAKES 12   **TOTAL TIME: 1 HR**

These pecan cookies came to us from Carolyn of the blog *All Day I Dream About Food* (alldayidreamaboutfood.com). They're a favorite in her family, and we can see why.

FOR COOKIES
2 cups almond flour
1 cup finely chopped pecans
2 tablespoons coconut flour
½ teaspoon baking powder
¼ teaspoon kosher salt
½ cup (1 stick) butter, softened
⅔ cup brown Swerve (or Swerve granular and 2 teaspoons yacon syrup)
1 large egg
½ teaspoon pure vanilla extract

FOR VANILLA GLAZE
⅔ cup Swerve confectioners or powdered erythritol
6 to 8 tablespoons heavy cream
½ teaspoon pure vanilla extract

1. Make cookies: Preheat oven to 325° and line two baking sheets with parchment paper. In a medium bowl, whisk together almond flour, pecans, coconut flour, baking powder, and salt.

2. In a large bowl, beat butter with sweetener until light and fluffy, about 2 minutes. Beat in egg and vanilla. Beat in almond flour mixture until dough comes together.

3. Form dough into ¾–inch balls, then roll between palms and shape into crescents. Place on prepared baking sheets.

4. Bake until just lightly golden brown, 15 to 18 minutes. (They will not be firm to the touch but will firm up as they cool.) Cool on baking sheets.

5. Make glaze: In a small bowl, whisk together sweetener with ¼ cup cream and vanilla until smooth. Add 1 tablespoon extra cream at a time until a thin but spreadable consistency is achieved. Spread on cooled cookies and decorate as desired.

NUTRITION (per serving):

170 calories
3 g protein
17 g carbohydrates
4 g fiber
1 g sugar
16 g fat
5 g saturated fat
45 mg sodium
11 g sugar alcohol

NUTRITION (per serving):

153 calories
2 g protein
7 g carbohydrates
2 g fiber
1 g sugar
15 g fat
10 g saturated fat
95 mg sodium
3 g sugar alcohol

SNICKERDOODLE SHORTBREAD

 MAKES 10   **TOTAL TIME: 1 HR 5 MIN**

They may look simple, maybe even a little boring, but they taste like a snickerdoodle went on a tropical vacation and therefore couldn't be anymore the opposite.

⅔ cup almond flour
⅓ cup coconut flour
¼ cup Swerve confectioners
1½ teaspoons ground cinnamon
½ teaspoon cream of tartar
½ teaspoon kosher salt
½ cup coconut oil, melted
1 teaspoon pure vanilla extract
3 tablespoons unsweetened shredded coconut

1. Preheat oven to 350° and line a large baking sheet with parchment paper.

2. In a medium bowl, whisk together flours, sweetener, cinnamon, cream of tartar, and salt. Add coconut oil and vanilla and stir until combined.

3. Shape dough into a ball, then transfer to a large piece of parchment paper. Cover with another piece of parchment and roll to ⅓–inch thickness. Transfer to refrigerator to chill for 15 minutes.

4. When dough is chilled, remove from refrigerator and use a cookie cutter to cut into 2–inch rounds. Roll edges in shredded coconut and place ½ inch apart on prepared baking sheet.

5. Bake until slightly golden around the edges, 12 to 15 minutes. Let cool completely.

ALMOND THUMBPRINTS

 MAKES 16   **TOTAL TIME: 1 HR 10 MIN**

This buttery cookie base tastes amazing with just about any kind of jam filling. Strawberry, raspberry, blackberry... the world is your thumbprint cookie.

4 tablespoons butter, softened
3 ounces cream cheese, softened
½ cup Swerve granular
1 large egg
1 teaspoon pure vanilla extract
¼ teaspoon kosher salt
1⅔ cups almond flour
8 teaspoons sugar-free jam

1. Preheat oven to 350° and line a large baking sheet with parchment paper.

2. In a large bowl using a hand mixer, mix together butter, cream cheese, and sweetener until completely combined. Add egg, vanilla, and salt and beat until combined, then beat in almond flour. Refrigerate dough for 20 minutes.

3. Using a 1-inch cookie dough scoop, scoop dough into balls and place at least 1 inch apart on prepared baking sheet. Use your thumb to make an indent in center of each cookie, then fill each indent with ½ teaspoon jam.

4. Bake until golden on bottom, 20 to 22 minutes. Let cool completely on baking sheet before serving.

PRO TIP!
If dough sticks to your thumb, dip in cold water before making indents, repeating as necessary.

NUTRITION (per serving):

126 calories
3 g protein
12 g carbohydrates
3 g fiber
1 g sugar
11 g fat
3 g saturated fat
76 mg sodium
8 g sugar alcohol

NUTRITION (per serving):

93 calories
3 g protein
9 g carbohydrates
2 g fiber
0.42 g sugar
8 g fat
3 g saturated fat
44 mg sodium
0 g sugar alcohol

CHOCOLATE CHIP COOKIES

 MAKES 18   **TOTAL TIME: 30 MIN**

When developing this recipe, our goal was to create an extra-chewy chocolate chip cookie, and we failed in that sense. The crumb of this cookie is far more delicate. But we fell in love with our "failure" nonetheless. It's the perfect amount of sweet and just as delicious when dunked in a glass of ice cold milk.

2 large eggs
½ cup (1 stick) melted butter
2 tablespoons heavy cream
2 teaspoons pure vanilla extract
2¾ cups almond flour
¼ teaspoon kosher salt
¼ cup Swerve granular
¾ cup sugar-free dark chocolate chips
Cooking spray

1. Preheat oven to 350°. In a large bowl, whisk egg with butter, heavy cream, and vanilla. Stir in almond flour, salt, and sweetener.

2. Fold in chocolate chips. Form dough into 1-inch balls and arrange 3 inches apart on parchment-lined baking sheets. Flatten balls with bottom of a glass that has been lightly greased with cooking spray.

3. Bake until cookies are golden, about 17 to 19 minutes.

WALNUT SNOWBALL COOKIES

 MAKES 15　　 **TOTAL TIME: 1 HR 5 MIN**

Rich and crumbly, just like a traditional snowball cookie, these bite-size treats are perfect for the holidays.

½ cup (1 stick) butter, melted
1 large egg
50 drops liquid stevia (about ¼ teaspoon)
½ teaspoon pure vanilla extract
1 cup walnuts
½ cup coconut flour, plus 1 to 2 tablespoons more for rolling
½ cup Swerve confectioners, divided

1. Preheat oven to 300° and line a baking sheet with parchment paper. In a large bowl, whisk together melted butter, egg, stevia, and vanilla.

2. To a food processor, add walnuts and pulse until ground. In a medium bowl, pour walnut flour, coconut flour, and ¼ cup sweetener and stir until combined.

3. In two parts, add dry mixture to wet and whisk to combine. At this point dough should be soft but firm enough to form into balls by hand without it sticking to your palms. If it is not right consistency, add 1 to 2 tablespoons of coconut flour and combine.

4. Make 15 equal-size balls and arrange on prepared baking sheet. Bake for 30 minutes until cookies are set. (They will not spread!)

5. Allow to cool for 5 minutes, and then roll still warm balls in remaining ¼ cup sweetener.

6. Place them on parchment paper and allow to fully cool, another 20 to 30 minutes, before eating.

NUTRITION (per serving):

122 calories
2 g protein
8 g carbohydrates
2 g fiber
1 g sugar
11 g fat
5 g saturated fat
16 mg sodium
5 g sugar alcohol

COOKIE SWAP | 39

NUTRITION (per serving):

185 calories
5 g protein
11 g carbohydrates
2 g fiber
1 g sugar
18 g fat
6 g saturated fat
51 mg sodium
7 g sugar alcohol

LEMON COOKIES

 MAKES 12   **TOTAL TIME: 55 MIN**

When life gives you lemons, make iced lemon cookies. They'll make your day a whole lot sweeter.

FOR COOKIES
½ cup (1 stick) butter, softened
⅓ cup Swerve confectioners
1 large egg
¼ cup lemon juice
Zest of 1 large lemon
2 cups blanched almond flour
¼ teaspoon kosher salt

FOR GLAZE
½ cup Swerve confectioners
2 tablespoons lemon juice

1. Preheat oven to 350° and line a medium baking sheet with parchment paper.

2. Make cookies: In a large bowl using a hand mixer, beat butter and sweetener until light and fluffy, about 2 minutes. Add egg and beat until combined, then add lemon juice and zest and beat until combined.

3. Add almond flour and salt and beat until combined. Cover surface of dough with plastic wrap and chill in refrigerator for 15 minutes.

4. Using a medium cookie scoop, scoop 12 evenly sized cookies, placing them at least 1 inch apart on prepared baking sheet. Press cookies down slightly using palm of hand.

5. Bake until cookies are golden on bottom, about 16 to 18 minutes. Let cool completely before glazing.

6. Make glaze: In a small bowl, whisk together sweetener and lemon juice until smooth. Drizzle glaze over cooled cookies.

DOUBLE CHOCOLATE COOKIES

 MAKES 11   **TOTAL TIME: 25 MIN**

This cookie, developed by blogger Joe Duff of *The Diet Chef* (thedietchefs.com), speaks to the inner chocoholic in all of us.

- 2½ tablespoons butter
- 3 tablespoons sugar-free chocolate chips, divided
- 1 large egg
- 1 teaspoon pure vanilla extract
- ⅔ cup blanched almond flour
- ⅓ cup Swerve confectioners
- 3½ tablespoons dark unsweetened cocoa powder
- ½ teaspoon baking powder
- Pinch kosher salt

1. Preheat oven to 325°. Line a baking sheet with parchment paper. In a medium microwave-safe bowl, combine butter and 1½ tablespoons chocolate chips. Microwave for 15 to 30 seconds, just enough to slightly melt butter and chocolate. Mix together until a chocolate sauce forms.

2. In a small bowl, whisk egg thoroughly. Then add egg and vanilla to chocolate sauce. Mix again.

3. Add remaining dry ingredients, saving some chocolate chips to top cookies. Mix until a ball of chocolate cookie dough forms.

4. Use a cookie scoop (or a tablespoon) to form 11 equal-size cookies. Place cookies on baking sheet and top each with remaining chocolate chips. Flatten each cookie with a spoon or spatula.

5. Bake for 8 to 10 minutes. (They should be VERY soft when they come out of the oven; but don't worry, this is normal!)

6. Let cool completely before serving. Store leftovers in an air-tight container in fridge.

NUTRITION (per serving):

96 calories
3 g protein
9 g carbohydrates
2 g fiber
0 g sugar
8 g fat
3 g saturated fat
44 mg sodium
4 g sugar alcohol

COOKIE SWAP | 43

NUTRITION (per serving):

120 calories
2 g protein
2 g carbohydrates
1 g fiber
0 g sugar
13 g fat
8 g saturated fat
25 mg sodium
7 g sugar alcohol

44 | KETO FOR DESSERT LOVERS

MAGIC COOKIES

MAKES 15 | **TOTAL TIME: 35 MIN**

You know those super-sweet magic bars with graham crackers, sweetened condensed milk, coconut, and chocolate? These magically taste like those. But without the carbs and sugar, of course.

¼ cup coconut oil
3 tablespoons butter, softened
3 tablespoons Swerve granular
½ teaspoon kosher salt
4 large egg yolks
1 cup sugar-free dark chocolate chips
1 cup coconut flakes
¾ cup roughly chopped walnuts

1. Preheat oven to 350° and line a baking sheet with parchment paper. In a large bowl, stir together coconut oil, butter, sweetener, salt, and egg yolks. Mix in chocolate chips, coconut, and walnuts.

2. Drop batter by the spoonful onto prepared baking sheet and bake until golden, 15 minutes.

3. Bake until cookies are golden, about 17 to 19 minutes.

BREAKFAST COOKIES

 MAKES 12   **TOTAL TIME: 45 MIN**

They say that breakfast is the most important meal of the day. So we say, make it count. Start the day with a peanut butter coconut raspberry cookie.

⅓ cup Swerve granular

2 large eggs

1 cup creamy sugar-free peanut butter

1 teaspoon pure vanilla extract

½ teaspoon baking soda

¼ teaspoon ground cinnamon

⅛ teaspoon kosher salt

½ cup unsweetened coconut flakes

½ cup thinly sliced almonds

½ cup chopped pecans

¼ cup sunflower seeds

2 teaspoons chia seeds

¾ cup unsweetened freeze-dried raspberries

1. Preheat oven to 350° and line a rimmed baking sheet with parchment paper.

2. In a medium bowl, whisk together sweetener and eggs until well combined. Stir in peanut butter, vanilla, baking soda, cinnamon, and salt. Stir vigorously until well combined, about 30 seconds.

3. Stir in coconut flakes, almonds, pecans, sunflower seeds, and chia seeds. Fold in freeze-dried raspberries.

4. Measure out level ¼ cups of dough, pressing to make sure it is firmly packed. Roll each ¼ cup into 1½-inch balls and press into a ¾-inch-thick disc. Evenly space on prepared baking sheet. Bake until slightly puffed and lightly golden, 12 to 15 minutes. Let cool completely.

NUTRITION (per serving):

254 calories
8 g protein
15 g carbohydrates
5 g fiber
2 g sugar
20 g fat
4 g saturated fat
156 mg sodium
5 g sugar alcohol

COOKIE SWAP | 47

NUTRITION (per serving):

118 calories
3 g protein
8 g carbohydrates
2 g fiber
1 g sugar
10 g fat
3 g saturated fat
190 mg sodium
4 g sugar alcohol

PEANUT BUTTER SANDIES

 MAKES 15   **TOTAL TIME: 40 MIN**

Are these keto? Yep, they are—but you wouldn't know it just by tasting them. They were a clear winner among lovers of peanut butter and fans of sandies: the crumbly texture comes naturally from the almond flour.

4 tablespoons butter, softened
⅓ cup Swerve granular
½ cup natural unsweetened peanut butter
1 large egg yolk
½ cup almond flour
1 tablespoon coconut flour
¼ teaspoon kosher salt, plus more for sprinkling
2 tablespoons finely chopped pecans, for topping

1. Preheat oven to 350° and line a large baking sheet with parchment paper.

2. In a medium bowl, using a whisk or hand mixer, cream together butter and sweetener until light and fluffy. Add peanut butter and whisk until completely incorporated. Whisk in yolk until fully combined. Fold in almond flour, coconut flour, and salt and mix until dough slightly stiffens.

3. Using a small cookie scoop, scoop dough 1 inch apart onto prepared sheet. Sprinkle cookies with more salt and pecans.

4. Bake until bottoms are deeply golden, about 11 minutes.

5. Cool completely before serving.

COPYCAT OREOS

 MAKES 12   **TOTAL TIME: 3 HR**

When our associate food editor Makinze said she wanted to recreate America's sandwich cookie, we had our doubts. But we were happily proven wrong. The secret? Black cocoa powder. It gives the cookies their iconic dark color and rich chocolate flavor.

FOR COOKIES
¾ cup almond flour
⅓ cup black cocoa powder
⅓ cup Swerve granular
2 tablespoons coconut flour
1 teaspoon kosher salt
½ teaspoon (gluten-free) baking powder
⅓ cup vegetable oil
1 large egg
1 teaspoon pure vanilla extract

FOR FILLING
½ cup (1 stick) butter, softened
¾ cup Swerve confectioners
1 teaspoon pure vanilla extract

1. Make cookies: In a large bowl, mix together almond flour, cocoa powder, sweetener, coconut flour, salt, and baking powder. Add oil, egg, and vanilla and mix until combined. Shape into a disc, then wrap in plastic wrap and refrigerate until firm, 2 hours.

2. Preheat oven to 350° and line a large baking sheet with parchment paper. Lightly dust a clean surface with cocoa powder and roll out dough ¼ inch thick. Cut out cookies with a 2-inch round cookie cutter.

3. Place cookies on prepared baking sheet. Bake until slightly firm to the touch, about 14 to 16 minutes. Let cool.

4. Make filling: In a large bowl using a hand mixer, beat butter until smooth. Add confectioners sweetener and beat until combined, then mix in vanilla. Roll into balls and press into a ¾-inch-thick disc. Evenly space on prepared baking sheet. Bake until slightly puffed and lightly golden, 12 to 15 minutes. Let cool completely.

5. Spread filling on one side of cookie and place a second cookie on top. Repeat with remaining cookies.

NUTRITION (per serving):

182 calories
3 g protein
19 g carbohydrates
3 g fiber
0.42 g sugar
18 g fat
6 g saturated fat
226 mg sodium
14 g sugar alcohol

CHAPTER THREE
POWER BARS

BERRY CRUMBLE BARS

 MAKES 9   **TOTAL TIME: 1 HR 15 MIN**

When summer rolls around, these bars are all we want. The combo of the (absolutely stunning) blueberry filling and the crumb topping gets us every single time.

FOR CRUST AND CRUMBLE
2½ cups almond flour
¼ cup coconut flour
¼ cup Swerve granular
¼ teaspoon kosher salt
¾ cup (1½ sticks) butter, melted
1 teaspoon pure vanilla extract
⅓ cup sliced almonds

FOR FILLING
3 cups blueberries, divided
Zest and juice of ½ lemon
¼ cup Swerve granular
1 tablespoon water
½ teaspoon xanthan gum

1. Preheat oven to 350° and line a 9-inch pan with parchment paper, leaving a 2-inch overhang.

2. Make the crust and crumble: In a large bowl, whisk together almond flour, coconut flour, sweetener, and salt. Add melted butter and vanilla and stir until a dough forms. Reserve 1 cup of mixture for topping.

3. Press remaining dough into prepared pan until smooth. Bake until lightly golden, 15 minutes.

4. Make the filling: In a small saucepan over medium heat, combine 2 cups blueberries, lemon zest and juice, sweetener, and water. Simmer until most blueberries have burst, 5 minutes. Spoon about 3 tablespoons blueberry liquid into a small bowl (it's okay if some blueberries get in there) and whisk in xanthan gum. Add to saucepan and continue to simmer until thickened, 2 to 3 minutes more. Remove from heat and stir in remaining 1 cup blueberries. Pour over crust.

5. Sprinkle almonds on top then crumble reserved dough on top. Bake until golden and blueberries are bubbly, 15 to 20 minutes. Let cool completely before removing from pan and cutting into squares.

PRO TIP! Swap in 3 cups raspberries, blackberries, or chopped strawberries for the blueberries.

NUTRITION (per serving):

385 calories
8 g protein
29 g carbohydrates
9 g fiber
7 g sugar
34 g fat
11 g saturated fat
73 mg sodium
11 g sugar alcohol

**NUTRITION
(per serving):**

232 calories
7 g protein
10 g carbohydrates
4 g fiber
1 g sugar
22 g fat
5 g saturated fat
80 mg sodium
4 g sugar alcohol

SNICKERDOODLE BLONDIES

 MAKES 16   **TOTAL TIME: 1 HR 10 MIN**

We have a very carb-filled, non-keto version of this recipe that will always have a special place in our hearts. This recipe was born out of our obsession with it. And while it doesn't taste quite like the original, we love it just the same.

½ cup (1 stick) butter, melted and slightly cooled, plus more for brushing
4 cups blanched finely ground almond flour
¼ cup packed brown Swerve
1 teaspoon baking powder
1½ teaspoons ground cinnamon, divided
¼ teaspoon kosher salt
2 large eggs
1 teaspoon pure vanilla extract
1 tablespoon Swerve granular

1. Preheat oven to 350°. Brush a 9x9-inch baking pan with butter. Line with parchment paper leaving a 2-inch overhang on two sides. Brush parchment with butter.

2. In a large bowl, combine almond flour and sweetener. Use your fingers to break up any clumps. Then add baking powder, ½ teaspoon cinnamon, and salt and whisk until well combined. Add butter, eggs, and vanilla and stir until well combined.

3. Scrape dough into prepared baking pan and, using a spatula, smooth into an even layer. Bake until golden and a toothpick inserted in center comes out clean, about 25 to 28 minutes. Let cool completely.

4. In a small bowl, combine remaining 1 teaspoon cinnamon and sweetener. Brush top of blondie lightly with butter and sprinkle all over with cinnamon-sweetener mixture.

SNICKERS BARS

 MAKES 40   **TOTAL TIME: 2 HR**

We're going to tell it to you straight. Homemade candy takes time and patience, especially when you're making caramel and nougat. But it's worth it 1,000 times over when you take a bite and realize that it's even better than the store-bought packaged candy.

FOR NOUGAT
1 cup raw cashews
Boiling water
1 cup blanched finely ground almond flour
½ cup coconut oil, melted, plus more for brushing
¼ cup finely shredded dried coconut
2 tablespoons Swerve granular
1 teaspoon pure vanilla extract
Kosher salt

FOR CARAMEL
¼ cup heavy cream
2 tablespoons brown Swerve
1 cup unsweetened natural creamy peanut butter
3 tablespoons coconut oil
2 tablespoons sugar-free maple syrup
2 teaspoons pure vanilla extract
Kosher salt
1½ cups salted roasted peanuts

FOR CHOCOLATE COATING
3 cups sugar-free semisweet chocolate chips
2 tablespoons coconut oil

1. Make nougat: In a large heatproof bowl, place cashews and pour enough boiling water over them to cover by at least 1 inch. Let sit 10 minutes. Drain well.

2. Transfer drained cashews to a blender. Add almond flour, coconut oil, dried coconut, sweetener, vanilla, and a pinch of salt. Process until smooth.

3. Brush a 9x9-inch baking pan with coconut oil. Line with parchment, leaving an overhang of at least 2 inches on two sides. Brush parchment with coconut oil. Scrape cashew mixture into prepared pan and spread into an even layer with a spatula. Transfer to freezer while making caramel layer.

4. Make caramel: In a large bowl, whisk heavy cream and sweetener until sweetener is dissolved and cream forms firm peaks. Add peanut butter, coconut oil, maple syrup, vanilla, and a pinch of salt and stir until well combined.

5. Scrape caramel mixture on top of nougat layer and spread evenly. Sprinkle evenly with peanuts and press lightly to partially submerge peanuts. Return to freezer and freeze until cold and firm, at least 1 hour.

6. Carefully lift frozen nougat and caramel layers from baking pan to a cutting board. Cut square into 4 long rectangles, then cut each rectangle crosswise into 10 bars.

7. Make chocolate coating: In a medium microwave-safe bowl, combine chocolate chips and coconut oil. Microwave, stirring every 20 seconds, until smooth.

8. Dip each bar in melted chocolate, then place on parchment-lined baking sheet. Place in refrigerator to set, 10 minutes.

NUTRITION (per serving):

233 calories
5 g protein
16 g carbohydrates
3 g fiber
1 g sugar
19 g fat
9 g saturated fat
45 mg sodium
1 g sugar alcohol

POWER BARS | 59

NUTRITION (per serving):

160 calories
4 g protein
15 g carbohydrates
5 g fiber
0.5 g sugar
14 g fat
5 g saturated fat
258 mg sodium
8 g sugar alcohol

AVOCADO BROWNIES

 MAKES 16   **TOTAL TIME: 1 HR 20 MIN**

These brownies have peanut butter and avocado in them. But truthfully, it's hard to tell. Both ingredients lend a smooth, fudgy texture, plus add a bunch of healthy fats, and that's all that really matters.

4 large eggs
2 ripe avocados
½ cup (1 stick) butter, melted
6 tablespoons unsweetened peanut butter
2 teaspoons baking soda
⅔ cup Swerve granular
⅔ cup unsweetened cocoa powder
2 teaspoons pure vanilla extract
½ teaspoon kosher salt
Flaky sea salt (optional)

1. Preheat oven to 350° and line an 8x8–inch square pan with parchment paper. In a blender or food processor, combine all ingredients except flaky sea salt and blend until smooth.

2. Transfer batter to prepared baking pan and smooth top with a spatula. Top with flaky sea salt (if using).

3. Bake until brownies are soft but not at all wet to the touch, 25 to 30 minutes.

4. Let cool 25 to 30 minutes before slicing and serving.

BUCKEYE BROWNIES

 MAKES 16   **TOTAL TIME: 1 HR 30 MIN**

Swirling the peanut butter cheesecake mixture into the brownie not only creates the most mesmerizing swirls, but it's extremely therapeutic. And easy! Neither artistic nor kitchen skills are required.

FOR PEANUT BUTTER MIXTURE
6 ounces cream cheese, softened
¼ cup Swerve confectioners
¼ cup sugar-free creamy peanut butter
1 large egg, at room temperature
¼ teaspoon kosher salt

FOR BROWNIE BATTER
½ cup (1 stick) butter, melted
⅔ cup Swerve confectioners
⅔ cup unsweetened cocoa powder
½ teaspoon kosher salt
3 large eggs, at room temperature
¾ cup almond flour

1. Preheat oven to 350° and line an 8x8-inch square baking pan with parchment paper.

2. Make peanut butter mixture: In a small microwave-safe bowl, microwave peanut butter until melted. In a large bowl, combine cream cheese and sweetener and beat until smooth. Add melted peanut butter, egg, and salt, and beat until combined.

3. Make brownie batter: In a large bowl, combine melted butter, sweetener, cocoa powder, and salt and beat until combined. Let cool slightly if mixture is warm.

4. Add eggs one at a time, whisking to incorporate. Add almond flour and mix until incorporated.

5. Pour ¾ brownie batter into prepared pan, then add peanut butter mixture in an even layer on top. Dollop with remaining brownie batter and use a butter knife to swirl the two batters.

6. Bake until peanut butter layer is set but slightly jiggly, 23 to 25 minutes. Let cool completely before slicing into squares and serving.

NUTRITION (per serving):

171 calories

5 g protein

13 g carbohydrates

2 g fiber

1 g sugar

16 g fat

7 g saturated fat

157 mg sodium

8 g sugar alcohol

POWER BARS | 63

NUTRITION (per serving):

371 calories
7 g protein
28 g carbohydrates
12 g fiber
2 g sugar
33 g fat
14 g saturated fat
237 mg sodium
5 g sugar alcohol

COOKIE DOUGH BARS

 MAKES 20   **TOTAL TIME: 2 HR 30 MIN**

Can we all agree that the best part of making cookies is the cookie dough? These bars celebrate this irrefutable fact. (You know it's true.)

---

1 cup (2 sticks) butter, softened
⅔ cup Swerve confectioners
1 teaspoon pure vanilla extract
1½ teaspoons kosher salt
4 cups almond flour
3 cups sugar-free dark chocolate chips, divided
Cooking spray
2 tablespoons coconut oil
Flaky sea salt

1. In a large bowl using a hand mixer, beat butter, sweetener, vanilla, and salt until light and fluffy. Slowly beat in almond flour until no dry spots remain, then fold in 1 cup of chocolate chips.

2. Coat an 8x8-inch baking pan with cooking spray. Line with parchment, leaving an overhang on two sides. Coat parchment with cooking spray. Spread cookie dough evenly into pan.

3. In a medium microwave-safe bowl, combine remaining 2 cups chocolate chips and coconut oil. Microwave, stirring every 30 seconds, until smooth and pourable. Pour chocolate over cookie dough layer and smooth. Garnish with flaky sea salt and place in freezer until set, about 30 minutes.

4. When ready to serve, remove from baking dish and cut into bars.

SAMOA BARS

 MAKES 16   **TOTAL TIME: 1 HR 35 MIN**

When you can't have Girl Scout cookies, you make a damn good alternative. If you have a soft spot for the kind in the purple box, these do not disappoint.

FOR CRUST
Cooking spray
2 cups almond flour
¼ cup Swerve confectioners
¼ teaspoon kosher salt
½ cup (1 stick) butter, melted

FOR FILLING
¼ cup (½ stick) butter
⅔ cup Swerve confectioners
½ cup heavy cream
1 teaspoon pure vanilla extract
½ teaspoon kosher salt
1½ cups toasted unsweetened shredded coconut
½ cup sugar-free dark chocolate chips
1 tablespoon coconut butter

1. Preheat oven to 350° and line a 9x9-inch baking pan with parchment paper and grease with cooking spray.

2. Make crust: In a large bowl, whisk together almond flour, sweetener, and salt. Add melted butter and stir to combine.

3. Press mixture into prepared pan in an even layer and bake until lightly golden, 18 to 20 minutes.

4. Meanwhile, make filling: In a small saucepan over medium-low heat, melt butter. When butter has melted and foam has subsided, stir in sweetener, cream, vanilla, and salt. Bring mixture up to a low simmer and cook, untouched, for 15 minutes.

5. When 15 minutes is up, transfer caramel to a heat-proof bowl and add shredded coconut. Stir in coconut and transfer to baked shortbread crust. Smooth into an even layer, let cool until softened, then transfer to refrigerator to firm up, 1 hour.

6. In a medium microwave-safe bowl, combine chocolate chips and coconut butter and microwave until melted. Stir to combine and drizzle over coconut. Chill 5 minutes in refrigerator, then cut into bars to serve.

NUTRITION (per serving):

271 calories
4 g protein
17 g carbohydrates
5 g fiber
2 g sugar
26 g fat
14 g saturated fat
99 mg sodium
8 g sugar alcohol

NUTRITION (per serving):

421 calories
10 g protein
23 g carbohydrates
6 g fiber
3 g sugar
40 g fat
15 g saturated fat
179 mg sodium
11 g sugar alcohol

KEY LIME PIE BARS

 MAKES 9   **TOTAL TIME: 3 HR 10 MIN**

We're going to let you in on a little-known secret. Keto key lime pie bars are better than traditional key lime pie. Mostly thanks to the cream cheese. It introduces a cheesecake vibe, and everyone, or at least anyone we care to be friends with, loves cheesecake.

FOR CRUST
- Cooking spray
- 2½ cups blanched finely ground almond flour
- 3 tablespoons Swerve granular
- 1 teaspoon key lime zest or lime zest
- ¼ teaspoon kosher salt
- ¼ cup (½ stick) butter, melted

FOR FILLING
- 4 ounces cream cheese, softened
- 1 cup heavy cream
- ¼ cup Swerve granular
- 4 large egg yolks
- ½ cup fresh key lime juice or lime juice
- ¼ teaspoon kosher salt

FOR TOPPING
- ¼ cup heavy cream
- 1 tablespoon plus 1 teaspoon Swerve confectioners
- 1 teaspoon pure vanilla extract
- Kosher salt
- Thinly sliced key lime rounds or thinly sliced half-moons of limes

1. Preheat oven to 350° and grease a 9x9-inch baking pan with cooking spray and line with parchment paper, leaving a 2-inch overhang on two opposing sides. Grease parchment with cooking spray.

2. Make crust: In a large bowl, whisk together almond flour, sweetener, lime zest, and salt. Pour in melted butter and stir to combine. Press mixture into prepared pan, using the back of a measuring cup to create an even layer. Bake until golden, about 15 minutes. Let cool on a wire rack.

3. Make filling: In a large bowl using a hand mixer, beat cream cheese until smooth. Add heavy cream, sweetener, egg yolks, lime juice, and salt and beat until combined. Pour filling over baked and cooled crust and bake until just set, about 25 to 30 minutes. Let cool to softened then cover with plastic and refrigerate until set, about 2 hours.

4. Make topping: In a medium bowl using a hand mixer, beat heavy cream, 1 teaspoon of sweetener, vanilla, and a pinch of salt until soft peaks form. Using a fine sieve, dust bars with remaining tablespoon sweetener. Cut bars into 9 squares and dollop each square with a small spoonful of whipped cream. Top with a lime round.

CHAPTER FOUR
CAKES & CUPCAKES

RED VELVET CAKE

 SERVES 12   **TOTAL TIME: 1 HR 45 MIN**

When it comes to birthday cakes, you're either on Team Funfetti (page 75), Team Chocolate (page 76), or Team Red Velvet. We're not saying any one of these options is better than the others…but we do get slightly more excited when the results of the latter are at a party.

FOR CAKE
Cooking spray
½ cup almond milk
2 tablespoons white distilled vinegar
3 cups almond flour
¼ cup Dutch process cocoa powder
1 teaspoon baking soda
½ teaspoon kosher salt
1 cup (2 sticks) butter, softened
¾ cup Swerve granular
3 large eggs
1 teaspoon pure vanilla extract
3 tablespoons red food coloring

FOR FROSTING
2 (8-ounce) blocks cream cheese, softened
½ cup (1 stick) butter, softened
1¼ cups Swerve confectioners
¼ cup heavy cream
1 teaspoon pure vanilla extract
Pinch of kosher salt

1. Preheat oven to 350°. Line two 8-inch round cake pans with parchment paper and grease with cooking spray. In a glass measuring cup or small bowl, combine almond milk and vinegar. Let sit at least 10 minutes.

2. In a medium bowl, whisk together almond flour, cocoa powder, baking soda, and salt.

3. In a large bowl using a hand mixer, beat butter and sweetener together. Add eggs one at a time until incorporated, then add vanilla. Add dry ingredients and mix until just combined. Add almond milk mixture and red food coloring and mix until just combined.

4. Divide batter evenly between prepared cake pans. Bake until a toothpick inserted in middle comes out clean, 35 to 40 minutes. Let cool 15 minutes, then flip onto a cooling rack and let cool completely.

5. Make frosting: In a large bowl using a hand mixer, beat cream cheese and butter until smooth. Add sweetener and beat until no lumps remain. Add heavy cream, vanilla, and a pinch of salt and beat until combined.

6. Place one cake layer on a serving platter and frost top with about ⅓ of frosting. Place second layer on top and frost top and sides with remaining frosting.

NUTRITION (per serving):

548 calories
11 g protein
39 g carbohydrates
6 g fiber
3 g sugar
54 g fat
25 g saturated fat
367 mg sodium
27 g sugar alcohol

NUTRITION (per serving):

561 calories
13 g protein
39 g carbohydrates
13 g fiber
4 g sugar
51 g fat
25 g saturated fat
367 mg sodium
15 g sugar alcohol

FUNFETTI BIRTHDAY CAKE

 SERVES 16   **TOTAL TIME: 2 HR 30 MIN**

Making your own sprinkles (page 83) is extremely impressive and fun. But when you don't have the time or just don't want to (which is 1,000% okay by the way), try this clever coconut flake hack.

FOR CAKE
Cooking spray
Assorted gel food coloring
1⅔ cups coconut flakes, divided
3½ cups almond flour
¾ cup coconut flour
1 teaspoon baking powder
¾ teaspoon baking soda
¼ teaspoon kosher salt
1½ sticks butter, softened, plus more for brushing
½ cup Swerve granular
4 large eggs
8 large egg whites
2 teaspoons pure vanilla extract
1 cup unsweetened almond milk
2 teaspoons distilled white vinegar

FOR FROSTING
1 cup (2 sticks) butter, softened
1 (8-ounce) block cream cheese, softened
1 cup Swerve confectioners
2 tablespoons unsweetened cocoa powder
¼ teaspoon kosher salt
1½ cups sugar-free semisweet chocolate chips

1. Preheat oven to 350°. Line two 8-inch cake pans with parchment paper and grease with cooking spray.

2. Make cake: In bottom of a small bowl, stir together about 5 drops of a gel food coloring and ¾ teaspoon water. Add ⅓ cup coconut and stir until coconut flakes absorb color. Repeat in separate bowls with remaining coconut flakes and colors. Set aside.

3. In a medium bowl, whisk together almond flour, coconut flour, baking powder, baking soda, and salt.

4. In a large bowl, beat butter and sweetener until light and fluffy, about 2 minutes. Add eggs, egg whites, and vanilla. Beat until well combined and foamy, about 1 minute. Add dry ingredients to wet and beat to combine. Add almond milk and vinegar and beat until combined.

5. Add all but a spoonful of each color of coconut flakes; fold to combine. Divide batter between baking pans and smooth top. Bake until toothpick inserted into center of cakes comes out clean, 50 minutes. Let cool completely.

6. Make frosting: In a large bowl, beat butter, cream cheese, sweetener, cocoa powder, and salt until light and fluffy, about 2 minutes. In a microwave-safe bowl, microwave chocolate chips until just melted. Pour melted chocolate into butter mixture and beat until well combined.

7. Using a serrated knife, remove domed tops of cakes to even. Place one cake on a platter or cake stand. Spread 1½ cups frosting onto top of cake layer. Top with remaining cake; frost top and sides with remaining frosting. Sprinkle top of cake with reserved colored coconut.

CAKES & CUPCAKES | 75

CHOCOLATE CAKE

 SERVES 12   **TOTAL TIME: 1 HR 30 MIN**

When developing the perfect keto chocolate cake, we took some inspiration from one of our favorite baking queens: Ina Garten. No, the Barefoot Contessa doesn't follow a keto diet. But she does add brewed coffee to her chocolate cake batter, and trust us, it's a game changer.

FOR CAKE
Cooking spray
1½ cups almond flour
⅔ cup unsweetened cocoa powder
¾ cup coconut flour
¼ cup flaxseed meal
2 teaspoons baking powder
2 teaspoons baking soda
1 teaspoon kosher salt
½ cup (1 stick) butter, softened
¾ cup Swerve granular
4 large eggs
1 teaspoon pure vanilla extract
1 cup almond milk
⅓ cup strong brewed coffee

FOR BUTTERCREAM
2 (8-ounce) blocks cream cheese, softened
½ cup (1 stick) butter, softened
¾ cup Swerve confectioners
½ cup unsweetened cocoa powder
½ cup coconut flour
¼ teaspoon instant coffee powder
¾ cup heavy cream
Pinch kosher salt

1. Preheat oven to 350° and line two 8-inch pans with parchment and grease with cooking spray.

2. Make cake: In a large bowl, whisk together almond flour, cocoa powder, coconut flour, flaxseed meal, baking powder, baking soda, and salt.

3. In another large bowl, using a hand mixer, beat butter and sweetener together until light and fluffy. Add eggs, one at a time, then add vanilla. Add dry ingredients and mix until just combined then stir in milk and coffee.

4. Divide batter between prepared pans and bake until a toothpick inserted into middle comes out clean, 28 minutes. Let cool completely.

5. Make frosting: In a large bowl, with a hand mixer, beat cream cheese and butter together until smooth. Add sweetener, cocoa powder, coconut flour, and instant coffee and beat until no lumps remain. Add cream and a pinch of salt and beat until combined.

6. Place one cake layer on serving platter or cake stand then spread a thick layer of buttercream on top. Repeat with remaining layers then frost sides of cake.

7. Keep refrigerated until ready to serve.

NUTRITION (per serving):

515 calories
12 g protein
42 g carbohydrates
12 g fiber
4 g sugar
47 g fat
24 g saturated fat
665 mg sodium
21 g sugar alcohol

NUTRITION (per serving):

274 calories
7 g protein
21 g carbohydrates
4 g fiber
2 g sugar
26 g fat
9 g saturated fat
180 mg sodium
14 g sugar alcohol

CITRUS-GLAZED POUND CAKE

 SERVES 12   **TOTAL TIME: 2 HR**

Hot take: Almond extract is better than vanilla extract. It might not be as versatile (which is why you won't see it often in this book), but just a tiny little bit can add a very noticeable oomph factor to baked goods. Don't @ us until you try this pound cake.

FOR CAKE
Cooking spray
½ cup (1 stick) butter, softened
½ (8-ounce) block cream cheese, softened
½ cup Swerve granular
3 large eggs
½ teaspoon pure almond extract
2½ cups almond flour
1 teaspoon baking powder
½ teaspoon kosher salt

FOR GLAZE
½ cup Swerve confectioners
3 tablespoons heavy cream
1 tablespoon freshly squeezed orange juice
Zest of ½ orange

1. Make cake: Preheat oven to 325° and grease a loaf pan with cooking spray. In a large bowl using a hand mixer, beat butter and cream cheese together. Add sweetener and beat until combined. Add eggs and almond extract and beat until incorporated.

2. In a medium bowl, whisk together almond flour, baking powder, and salt. Add to wet ingredients and mix until just combined.

3. Pour batter into prepared pan and bake until golden and a toothpick inserted in middle comes out clean, about 1 hour 20 minutes. If top starts to get too dark, loosely cover with foil. Let cool 10 minutes then flip onto a cooling rack to let cool completely.

4. In a small bowl, mix together sweetener, heavy cream, orange juice, and zest. Pour over cooled cake. Let set for 10 minutes before slicing.

TIRAMISU CHAFFLE CAKE

 SERVES 6   **TOTAL TIME: 3 HR**

Let's talk chaffles. Chaffles are keto waffles made with cheese. And while they sound absolutely wild, they're insanely good all on their own. Stack them up and add a fluffy mascarpone tiramisu filling, and it's almost too much deliciousness to handle.

FOR CHAFFLES
4 large eggs
½ cup blanched finely ground almond flour
2 teaspoons pure vanilla extract
2 tablespoons Swerve granular
1 teaspoon baking soda
2 cups shredded mozzarella
Cooking spray

FOR FILLING
4 large egg yolks
¼ cup Swerve granular
16 ounces mascarpone cheese, softened
1½ cups heavy cream
1 teaspoon pure vanilla extract

FOR COCOA
1 tablespoon keto cocoa powder
1 teaspoon Swerve confectioners
¼ teaspoon instant espresso powder

1. Make chaffles: Preheat waffle iron to medium-high. In a large bowl, beat eggs. Whisk in almond flour, vanilla, sweetener, and baking soda until well combined. Stir in mozzarella.

2. Grease waffle iron with cooking spray, then pour a quarter of batter into waffle iron and cook until light golden, about 2 to 3 minutes. Let cool on a wire rack. Repeat 3 times.

3. Make filling: Bring a medium saucepan filled about 2 inches full with water to a simmer over medium heat. In a large heatproof bowl, combine egg yolks and sweetener and set over simmering pot. Whisking constantly, cook mixture over medium-low heat until doubled in volume and velvety smooth, about 5 minutes. Remove from heat and whisk in mascarpone cheese until smooth. Let cool slightly.

4. Meanwhile, in a large bowl, beat heavy cream and vanilla until stiff peaks form, about 5 minutes. Fold whipped cream into mascarpone custard just until combined. Set aside.

5. Make cocoa mixture: In a small bowl, whisk together cocoa, sweetener, and espresso powder.

6. On a large plate or platter, arrange one chaffle. Dust generously with cocoa powder mixture. Top with a quarter of filling, spread into an even layer, leaving about a ¼-inch border around edges. Repeat with remaining chaffles, filling, and cocoa powder.

7. Cover and refrigerate for 2 hours and up to overnight. Serve chilled.

NUTRITION (per serving):

791 calories
0 g protein
26 g carbohydrates
0 g fiber
5 g sugar
73 g fat
43 g saturated fat
563 mg sodium
13 g sugar alcohol

PRO TIP! These chaffles taste equally delicious layered with whipped cream and berries.

CAKES & CUPCAKES

NUTRITION (per serving):

8 calories
0 g protein
19 g carbohydrates
0 g fiber
1 g sugar
0 g fat
0 g saturated fat
13 mg sodium
18 g sugar alcohol

SPRINKLES

 SERVES 8   **TOTAL TIME: 4 HR 20 MIN**

Unfortunately, it's not easy to secure store-bought sugar-free rainbow sprinkles. But it is pretty freaking easy to make your own. You'll just need to plan ahead! They need at least 4 hours to dry.

1 cup Swerve confectioners
2 tablespoons meringue powder
1 tablespoon fresh lemon juice
Gel food coloring

1. Line three baking sheets with parchment paper. In a stand mixer fitted with the whisk attachment, whisk all ingredients with ¼ cup water on high speed until thick and white, about 7 minutes.

2. Depending on how many colors are desired, separate frosting into bowls. Add food coloring just a few drops at a time until desired color is achieved.

3. Scrape each colored mixture into a separate pastry bag fitted with a 1/16-inch round pastry tip or a squeeze bottle. Pipe very thin lines onto prepared baking sheets.

4. Let sprinkles air dry at least 4 hours but preferably overnight. It will take longer for colored sprinkles to dry. When dry, break sprinkles into desired size.

PSL CUPCAKES

MAKES 12 | **TOTAL TIME: 45 MIN**

If being basic means eating PSL cupcakes during autumn, we don't want to be anything else. Give us all the pumpkin spice, all fall long.

FOR CUPCAKES

Cooking spray
4 large eggs
¾ cup pure pumpkin puree
4 tablespoons butter, melted and slightly cooled
½ cup Swerve granular
2 teaspoons pure vanilla extract
2 cups blanched finely ground almond flour
3½ teaspoons pumpkin pie spice mix, plus more for sprinkling
1 teaspoon baking soda
½ teaspoon instant espresso powder, plus more for sprinkling
½ teaspoon kosher salt

FOR FROSTING

1½ (8-ounce) blocks cream cheese, softened
4 tablespoons (½ stick) butter, softened
⅓ cup Swerve confectioners
1 tablespoon heavy cream
½ teaspoon pure vanilla extract
Pinch of kosher salt

1. Preheat oven to 350°. Line a 12-cup muffin pan with cupcake liners. Spray liners with cooking spray.

2. Make cupcakes: In a large bowl, whisk together eggs, pumpkin, butter, sweetener, and vanilla. Add almond flour, pumpkin pie spice, baking soda, espresso powder, and salt to the wet ingredients and whisk well to combine, about 1 minute.

3. Scoop batter into cupcake papers, filling each ¾ way full. Firmly tap muffin pan on an even surface a few times to settle batter into an even layer.

4. Bake until a toothpick inserted into center of a cupcake comes out clean and cupcakes are set, about 30 minutes. Let cool completely.

5. Make frosting: In a large bowl using a hand mixer, beat cream cheese, butter, sweetener, heavy cream, vanilla, and salt until light and fluffy, about 3 minutes. Transfer frosting to a pastry bag fitted with a star tip.

6. Pipe frosting on top of cooled cupcakes and sprinkle with more pumpkin pie spice and espresso powder.

NUTRITION (per serving):

321 calories
8 g protein
24 g carbohydrates
6 g fiber
3 g sugar
30 g fat
12 g saturated fat
313 mg sodium
13 g sugar alcohol

NUTRITION (per serving):

715 calories
19 g protein
48 g carbohydrates
9 g fiber
6 g sugar
65 g fat
27 g saturated fat
527 mg sodium
28 g sugar alcohol

LEMON BLUEBERRY CAKE

 SERVES 8-10   **TOTAL TIME: 2 HR**

On the list of all-time great food pairings, lemon blueberry ranks very high. Somewhere extremely close to chocolate and peanut butter, which says *a lot*.

FOR CAKE
½ cup (1 stick) butter, melted plus more for brushing
4 cups blanched finely ground almond flour
½ cup coconut flour
½ cup Swerve granular
2 teaspoons baking powder
¾ teaspoon kosher salt
8 large eggs
1 teaspoon finely grated lemon zest
1 tablespoon lemon juice
1 tablespoon pure vanilla extract
1 cup fresh blueberries

FOR FROSTING
2 (8-ounce) blocks cream cheese, softened
½ cup (1 stick) butter, softened
1¼ cup Swerve confectioners
¼ cup heavy cream
3 tablespoons fresh lemon juice
1 teaspoon pure vanilla extract
¼ teaspoon kosher salt

FOR ASSEMBLY
½ thinly sliced lemon

1. Preheat oven to 350°. Brush two 9-inch round cake pans with melted butter. Line bottom with parchment. Brush parchment. Set aside.

2. Make cake: In a large bowl, whisk almond flour, coconut flour, sweetener, baking powder, and salt.

3. In another large bowl, whisk butter, eggs, lemon zest and juice, and vanilla until well combined. Stir dry ingredients into wet until well combined. Gently fold blueberries into batter.

4. Divide batter between prepared baking pans and smooth evenly in pans with spatula. Bake until golden around edges and a bit on top and a toothpick inserted in center comes out clean, 30 to 33 minutes. Remove to a wire rack and let cool completely.

5. Make frosting: In a large bowl, beat cream cheese, butter, sweetener, heavy cream, lemon juice, vanilla, and salt until light and fluffy, about 3 minutes.

6. Assemble cake: Remove cakes from pans and remove parchment from cakes. Trim tops from cake to create even layers. Place one cake on a large plate. Spread 1 cup of frosting evenly on top, then top with second cake. Spread remaining frosting on top and sides of cake, then arrange lemon in center of cake.

PERFECT BUTTERCREAM

 SERVES 12   **TOTAL TIME: 10 MIN**

Fact: Cream cheese frosting is the queen of all frostings. Thus, our classic vanilla buttercream calls for a good amount of it. And so does our chocolate buttercream, which is pretty much the same formula but with cocoa powder and a little espresso powder.

½ cup (1 stick) butter, softened
6 ounces cream cheese, softened
½ cup Swerve confectioners
2 teaspoons pure vanilla extract
¼ teaspoon kosher salt

In a large bowl, whisk together butter and cream cheese for 1 to 2 minutes. Add sweetener, vanilla, and salt and beat until combined.

PRO TIP! To make chocolate frosting, decrease vanilla extract to 1 teaspoon, and add 3 tablespoons unsweetened cocoa powder and ½ teaspoon espresso powder.

NUTRITION (per serving):

120 calories
1 g protein
7 g carbohydrates
0 g fiber
1 g sugar
13 g fat
8 g saturated fat
86 mg sodium
6 g sugar alcohol

CHAPTER FIVE
AMAZING CHEESECAKES

MINI CINNAMON ROLL CHEESECAKES

 SERVES 12   **TOTAL TIME: 1 HR 50 MIN**

Cinnamon roll lovers, you won't miss the fluffy carbs in these mini cheesecakes. We promise!

FOR CRUST
Cooking spray
1⅓ cups almond flour
¼ cup coconut flour
2 tablespoons Swerve granular
½ teaspoon cinnamon
¼ teaspoon kosher salt
7 tablespoons butter, melted

FOR FILLING
2 (8-ounce) blocks cream cheese, softened
¼ cup Swerve granular
2 large eggs
¼ cup sour cream
1 teaspoon pure vanilla extract
1 tablespoon plus ½ teaspoon cinnamon, divided
¼ teaspoon kosher salt
¼ cup brown Swerve

FOR FROSTING
4 ounces cream cheese, softened
4 tablespoons (½ stick) butter, softened
½ cup Swerve confectioners
2 tablespoons heavy cream
1 teaspoon pure vanilla extract
Pinch of kosher salt

1. Preheat oven to 350° and line a muffin pan with liners. Grease liners with cooking spray.

2. Make crust: In a small bowl, whisk together almond flour, coconut flour, sweetener, cinnamon, and salt. Add melted butter and mix until well combined. Divide mixture among liners, about 1½ tablespoons in each. Use a spoon to pack mixture into liners.

3. Bake until edges are lightly golden, 8 to 10 minutes. Let cool while you make cheesecake mixture.

4. Make filling: Lower oven temperature to 325°. In a large bowl using a hand mixer, beat cream cheese until smooth. Add sweetener and beat until no lumps remain. Add eggs, one at a time, and beat until combined. Add sour cream, vanilla, ½ teaspoon cinnamon, and salt.

5. In a small bowl, combine brown sweetener and remaining 1 tablespoon cinnamon.

6. Spoon about 1½ tablespoons cheesecake filling over each crust. Sprinkle about 1½ teaspoons brown sugar mixture over filling. Top with remaining filling.

7. Bake cheesecakes until just set in middle, 18 to 20 minutes. Refrigerate until well chilled and set, 2 hours.

8. Make frosting: In a large bowl using a hand mixer, beat cream cheese and butter until smooth. Add confectioners sweetener and beat until no lumps remain. Add heavy cream, vanilla, and a pinch of salt and beat until combined.

9. Transfer to a piping bag fitted with a small round tip and pipe frosting into a swirl over chilled cheesecakes.

NUTRITION (per serving):

377 calories
7 g protein
21 g carbohydrates
4 g fiber
3 g sugar
36 g fat
18 g saturated fat
261 mg sodium
12 g sugar alcohol

AMAZING CHEESECAKES

NUTRITION (per serving):

199 calories
5 g protein
24 g carbohydrates
6 g fiber
1 g sugar
18 g fat
8 g saturated fat
106 mg sodium
15 g sugar alcohol

CHEESECAKE-SWIRLED BROWNIES

 MAKES 16   **TOTAL TIME: 1 HR 15 MIN**

There's no occasion in which it wouldn't be appropriate to bring these marbled brownies. Birthday, piano recital, summer cookout, a much-owed apology, a desperate attempt at bribery...you get the picture.

FOR BROWNIE
Cooking spray
1½ cups blanched finely ground almond flour
1 cup Swerve granular
¾ cup keto cocoa powder
¾ teaspoon baking powder
⅛ teaspoon kosher salt
1 stick butter, melted, plus more for greasing
3 large eggs
¼ cup unsweetened almond milk
1 teaspoon pure vanilla extract

FOR CHEESECAKE SWIRL
1 (8-ounce) block cream cheese
¼ cup Swerve granular
1 large egg yolk
1 teaspoon pure vanilla extract

1. Preheat oven to 350° and grease a 9-inch square metal baking pan with cooking spray. Line with parchment paper, leaving an overhang on two sides. Spray parchment.

2. Make brownie: In a large bowl, whisk together almond flour, sweetener, cocoa powder, baking powder, and salt. Add butter, eggs, milk, and vanilla, and stir until very well combined, about 1 minute.

3. Make cheesecake swirl: In a medium microwave-safe bowl, melt cream cheese, about 45 seconds. Add sweetener, egg yolk, and vanilla. Whisk until smooth.

4. Scoop all but 1 cup of brownie batter into prepared pan, spreading it evenly to edges. Dollop with half of cheesecake mixture. Spoon remaining brownie batter over top in small dollops. Dollop with remaining half of cheesecake mixture. Use a butter knife to gently swirl brownie and cheesecake batters, creating a marble effect.

5. Bake until puffed and a toothpick inserted into center of brownies comes out with just a few crumbs. Edges might just begin to brown, about 30 to 35 minutes. Let cool completely on a wire rack. Slice into squares and serve.

AMAZING CHEESECAKES | 95

CLASSIC CHEESECAKE

 SERVES 8   **TOTAL TIME: 8 HR**

This crust is buttery and crumbly just like the graham cracker version but with tons more protein. The filling has three blocks of cream cheese and 16 ounces of sour cream. Because fat can be your friend.

FOR CRUST
Nonstick cooking spray
½ cup almond flour
½ cup coconut flour
¼ cup shredded coconut
½ cup (1 stick) butter, melted

FOR FILLING
3 (8-ounce) blocks cream cheese, softened
16 ounces sour cream, softened
1 tablespoon stevia
2 teaspoons pure vanilla extract
3 large eggs, at room temperature
1 cup sliced strawberries, for serving
1 cup blueberries, for serving

1. Preheat oven to 300° and grease an 8-inch or 9-inch springform pan with cooking spray. Cover bottom and edges with foil.

2. Make crust: In a medium bowl, mix together flours, coconut, and butter. Press crust into bottom and a little up sides of prepared pan. Place pan in fridge while you make filling.

3. Make filling: In a large bowl using a hand mixer, beat cream cheese and sour cream together then beat in stevia and vanilla. Add eggs one at a time, mixing after each addition. Spread filling evenly over crust.

4. Place cheesecake in a deep roasting pan and set on middle rack of oven. Carefully pour enough boiling water into roasting pan to come halfway up sides of springform pan. Bake for 1 hour to 1 hour 20 minutes, until it only slightly jiggles in center. Turn oven off, but leave cake in oven with door slightly ajar to cool slowly for an hour.

5. Remove pan from water bath and take off foil. Let chill in fridge for at least 5 hours or overnight. Slice and garnish with berries.

NUTRITION (per serving):

647 calories
12 g protein
18 g carbohydrates
5 g fiber
9 g sugar
60 g fat
34 g saturated fat
418 mg sodium
0 g sugar alcohol

NUTRITION (per serving):

226 calories
4 g protein
21 g carbohydrates
3 g fiber
2 g sugar
22 g fat
10 g saturated fat
103 mg sodium
16 g sugar alcohol

COOKIES 'N' CREAM CHEESECAKES

 MAKES 12   **TOTAL TIME: 4 HR 25 MIN**

Cookies 'n' cream is an undervalued flavor profile that deserves more dessert attention beyond just ice cream. Enter the cutest no-bake cheesecakes that, yeah, do kinda taste like ice cream.

FOR CRUST
1¼ cups almond flour
¼ cup Swerve granular
3 tablespoons unsweetened cocoa powder
Kosher salt
¼ cup (½ stick) butter, melted

FOR CHEESECAKE
6 ounces cream cheese, softened
1 cup Swerve confectioners
1 teaspoon pure vanilla extract
Kosher salt
1 cup cold heavy cream

1. Line a muffin pan with 12 cupcake liners.

2. Make crust: In a medium bowl, whisk together flour, sweetener, cocoa powder, and a pinch of salt. Add butter and stir until completely incorporated.

3. Add about 1 tablespoon crust mixture to each cupcake liner and press to compact crust into an even layer. Press remainder of crust into an even layer in mixing bowl and place in freezer while you make cheesecake mixture.

4. Make filling: In a large bowl using a hand mixer, beat together cream cheese and sweetener until completely combined. Add vanilla and salt and beat until fully incorporated.

5. In another large bowl using a hand mixer or whisk, beat heavy cream until stiff peaks form. With a rubber spatula, fold ¼ of whipped cream into cream cheese mixture until it is completely combined. Repeat three more times until all whipped cream is combined with cream cheese mixture.

6. Remove remaining crust mixture from freezer and crumble into bowl with cheesecake mixture, reserving about 2 tablespoons for topping. Divide mixture evenly among cupcake liners then top with remaining crust crumbles. Refrigerate until set, 4 hours. (Or, freeze until set—1 hour.)

RASPBERRY-SWIRLED CHEESECAKE BARS

 MAKES 9   **TOTAL TIME: 1 HR 10 MIN**

What we're about to say we know you've heard a million times before. We have, too, and we always roll our eyes. But it needs to be said. These are *almost* too pretty to eat.

FOR CRUST
Cooking spray
¾ cup almond flour
¼ cup coconut flour
¼ cup shredded unsweetened coconut
2 tablespoons Swerve granular
½ cup (1 stick) butter, melted
¼ teaspoon kosher salt

FOR RASPBERRY SWIRL
¾ cup raspberries
1 tablespoon Swerve granular

FOR FILLING
2 (8-ounce) blocks cream cheese, softened
½ cup Swerve confectioners
Zest of 1 lemon
2 tablespoons lemon juice
2 tablespoons heavy cream
2 large eggs

1. Preheat oven to 350° and line an 8x8-inch baking pan with parchment paper and grease with cooking spray.

2. Make crust: In a medium bowl, mix together almond flour, coconut flour, coconut, sweetener, butter, and salt. Press mixture into prepared pan.

3. Make raspberry swirl: Combine raspberries and sweetener in a food processor or blender and pulse until smooth. Strain mixture using a fine sieve.

4. Make filling: In a large bowl using a hand mixer, beat cream cheese with sweetener until fluffy, then beat in lemon zest, lemon juice, and heavy cream. Add eggs one at a time, mixing after each addition. Spread filling evenly over crust. Dollop spoonfuls of raspberry mixture over cheesecake, then use a toothpick to swirl into filling.

5. Bake until filling only slightly jiggles in center, 40 to 45 minutes. Turn oven off, but leave cake in oven with door slightly ajar to cool slowly for an hour.

6. Let cool to softened, then refrigerate until ready to serve. Just before serving, remove from pan, discard parchment, and cut into bars.

NUTRITION (per serving):

387 calories
7 g protein
21 g carbohydrates
4 g fiber
4 g sugar
37 g fat
20 g saturated fat
239 mg sodium
12 g sugar alcohol

NUTRITION (per serving):

411 calories
6 g protein
22 g carbohydrates
4 g fiber
4 g sugar
41 g fat
23 g saturated fat
359 mg sodium
12 g sugar alcohol

LEMON CHEESECAKE MOUSSE

 MAKES 4   **TOTAL TIME: 1 HR 30 MIN**

When baking a cheesecake is out of the question (because it's hot, or your springform pan is missing, or there's not enough time, or you just don't want to do it and, no, you don't need to explain yourself), make this. It's light, airy, and pretty freaking adorable.

FOR CRUMBLE
¼ cup blanched finely ground almond flour
1 tablespoon butter
1 teaspoon keto maple syrup
½ teaspoon ground cinnamon
Kosher salt

FOR MOUSSE
1 (8-ounce) block cream cheese, softened
¼ cup Swerve granular
3 tablespoons freshly squeezed lemon juice, plus finely grated zest for serving and 1 thin lemon round, quartered
½ teaspoon pure vanilla extract
¼ teaspoon kosher salt
⅔ cup heavy cream

1. Make crumble: Preheat oven to 350°. In a small bowl, combine almond flour, butter, maple syrup, cinnamon, and a large pinch of salt. Stir until mixture starts to clump. Scrape mixture onto a small baking sheet and use your fingers to break up into tiny clumps (pea size and smaller). Bake, until light golden, stirring halfway through, about 8 minutes. Let cool; it will crisp as it cools.

2. Make mousse: Meanwhile, in a large bowl using a hand mixer at medium-high speed, beat cream cheese, sweetener, lemon juice, vanilla, and salt until light and fluffy, about 2 minutes.

3. In another large bowl using a hand mixer at medium-high speed, beat heavy cream until firm peaks form.

4. Gently fold whipped cream into cream cheese mixture until just combined. Fill a piping bag fitted with a star tip with mousse.

5. Divide graham crumb between 4 dessert cups, breaking up any larger pieces with your fingers. Pipe cream cheese mixture into cups. Refrigerate until thickened, at least 1 hour or up to overnight covered.

6. Sprinkle with more graham crumb and lemon zest. Garnish with lemon.

PRO TIP! The "graham cracker" crumble adds a nice textural contrast to the fluffy mouse, but it's not necessary.

CHAPTER SIX

PIES & COBBLERS

POP TARTS

 MAKES 4   **TOTAL TIME: 3 HR**

Pop tarts are essentially just adorable mini hand pies. And though their ingredient list aligns more with the dessert category, we don't judge anyone who prefers to eat them for breakfast.

FOR CRUST
- 1½ cups almond flour
- 3 tablespoons coconut flour
- 1 tablespoon Swerve granular
- ¼ teaspoon xanthan gum
- ¼ teaspoon baking powder
- ¼ teaspoon kosher salt
- ½ cup (1 stick) cold butter, cubed
- 1 large egg, beaten
- ¼ cup sugar-free jam
- Egg wash, for brushing

FOR GLAZE
- ½ cup Swerve confectioners
- 2 tablespoons plus 1 teaspoon heavy cream
- 1 teaspoon pure vanilla extract

1. Make crust: In a food processor, pulse together almond flour, coconut flour, sweetener, xanthan gum, baking powder, and salt. Add butter and pulse until mostly pea-sized, then add egg and pulse just until incorporated. Remove from food processor and pat into a smooth flat disc and wrap in plastic wrap. Refrigerate until well chilled, at least 2 hours.

2. Place chilled dough between 2 pieces of parchment paper and roll into an 11-inch square, about ¼ inch thick. If dough cracks, pinch it back together. Place dough on a large baking sheet and place in freezer for 10 minutes.

3. Preheat oven to 350°. Cut dough into 8 rectangles that are about 2½ inches wide and 5½ inches long. Spoon 1 tablespoon jam onto each of 4 rectangles and spread into an even layer, leaving a ½-inch border around edges. Top with remaining 4 rectangles and use a fork to crimp edges. Return to freezer for 15 minutes. If dough starts to stick or is too warm, you can place back in freezer first before crimping.

4. Brush with an egg wash and bake until golden and edges start to feel firm, 20 to 25 minutes. Let cool completely.

5. Make glaze: In a small bowl, whisk together sweetener, heavy cream, and vanilla. Spread over center of cooled pop tarts.

NUTRITION (per serving):

570 calories
13 g protein
46 g carbohydrates
7 g fiber
4 g sugar
51 g fat
19 g saturated fat
211 mg sodium
33 g sugar alcohol

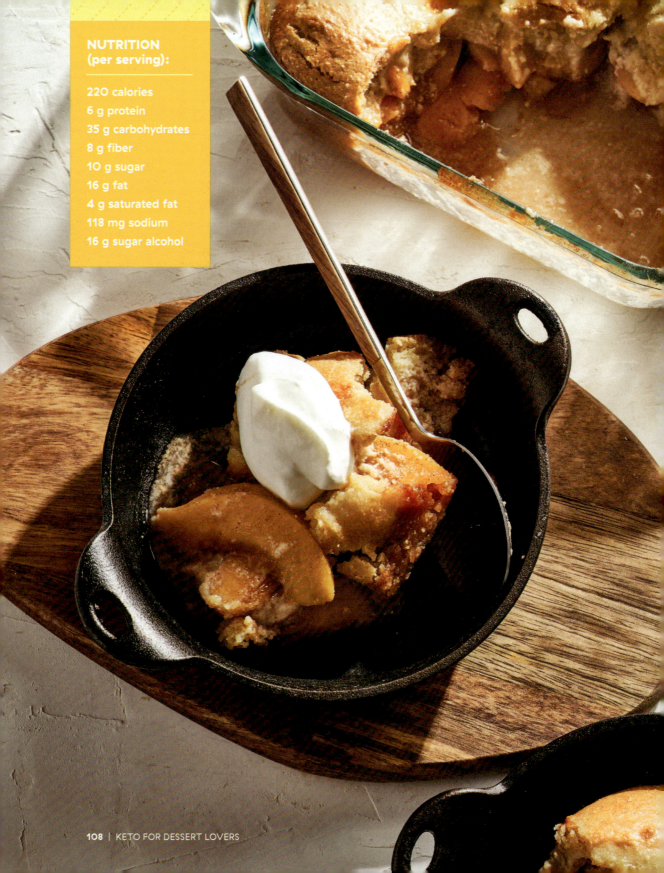

NUTRITION (per serving):

220 calories
6 g protein
35 g carbohydrates
8 g fiber
10 g sugar
16 g fat
4 g saturated fat
118 mg sodium
16 g sugar alcohol

PEACH COBBLER

 SERVES 9   **TOTAL TIME: 55 MIN**

It's as if peaches existed solely to be topped with this fluffy buttermilk biscuit topping. Seriously.

6 cups sliced peaches
Juice of ½ lemon
¾ cup Swerve granular, divided
1 teaspoon cinnamon
1½ cups almond flour
1½ teaspoons baking powder
4 tablespoons butter, melted
1 large egg
½ cup buttermilk
1 teaspoon pure vanilla extract

1. Preheat oven to 350°. In a large saucepan, combine peaches, lemon juice, ½ cup sweetener, and cinnamon. Heat peaches over medium-high heat until juices come to a boil. Reduce to a simmer and let reduce until juices are slightly syrupy, about 3 to 5 minutes. Set aside.

2. In a large bowl, whisk together almond flour, baking powder, and ¼ cup remaining sweetener until fully combined. Add butter, egg, buttermilk, and vanilla and mix until a slightly thick batter has formed.

3. Pour peaches into a 9x9-inch baking dish. Using a large spoon or ice cream scoop, dollop batter over peaches. Bake until fruit is bubbling and biscuits are golden, 40 to 45 minutes.

> **PRO TIP!**
> If you want to sub in frozen peaches, make sure they're defrosted first! (You can zap them in the microwave for 30-second intervals if you need to do so quickly.)

PIES & COBBLERS | 109

PERFECT PIE CRUST

 SERVES 8   **TOTAL TIME: 10 MIN**

By now, you probably get it. Mozzarella cheese is a key keto pastry ingredient. Embrace the weirdness, friends. Your pies will thank you.

- 1½ cups shredded mozzarella cheese
- 1 cup blanched finely ground almond flour
- 1 large egg, beaten
- 1½ teaspoons Swerve granular

1. Place mozzarella in a medium microwave-safe bowl. Microwave until mozzarella is melted, about 1 minute. Add almond flour, egg, and sweetener to bowl. Stir with a wooden spoon. Once dough starts to come together, knead dough with hands until fully combined, about 1 minute.

2. Dough is ready to use right away; do not rest. Dust surface with flour when rolling out. Make 2 discs for double-crusted pies and 1 disc is perfect for single-crust pies. Refrigerate for at least 5 hours or overnight. Slice and garnish with strawberries.

NUTRITION (per serving):

155 calories
8 g protein
4 g carbohydrates
0 g fiber
0 g sugar
13 g fat
4 g saturated fat
143 mg sodium
0 g sugar alcohol

PIES & COBBLERS

NUTRITION (per serving):

362 calories
18 g protein
24 g carbohydrates
7 g fiber
7 g sugar
27 g fat
7 g saturated fat
296 mg sodium
8 g sugar alcohol

BLUEBERRY PIE

 SERVES 8   **TOTAL TIME: 2 HR 30 MIN**

Though summer blueberries are obviously ideal, this recipe can transform even the blandest, mealiest berries into something spectacular.

3 cups fresh blueberries
¼ cup Swerve granular
½ teaspoon fresh lemon juice
1 tablespoon chia seeds
¼ teaspoon ground cinnamon
Blanched finely ground almond flour, for dusting
2 discs Perfect Pie Crust (page 110)
1 large egg, beaten

1. Preheat oven to 400°. In a large bowl, combine blueberries, sweetener, lemon juice, chia seeds, and cinnamon. Set aside.

2. On a lightly almond-floured surface, roll out one disc of keto pie crust to about an 11-inch circle, dusting lightly with more almond flour on both sides if dough begins to stick to either rolling pin or counter.

3. Carefully fit rolled-out pie dough into a 9-inch metal pie dish and fill crust with blueberry mixture, scraping any accumulated juices or sugar in bowl into pie dish with blueberry mixture.

4. Lightly almond-flour surface and roll second disc of pie dough to a 10-inch circle, lightly flouring with more almond flour as necessary. Cut dough into 10 strips, each about 1-inch wide.

5. Lay 5 strips across pie at even intervals, then weave remaining strips in and out to make a lattice crust. Press edges together to seal and then trim off or fold under any remaining dough. Crimp crust. Brush crust lightly with egg.

6. Bake 20 minutes, and then tent with foil and reduce heat to 375°. Continue to bake until fruit is bubbly and crust is golden brown, about 45 minutes more. Set aside to cool. Serve warm or at room temperature.

STRAWBERRY SHORTCAKE

 SERVES 4   **TOTAL TIME: 1 HR**

Shortcakes (aka biscuits) + macerated strawberries + whipped cream = one of life's greatest desserts. Even without the carbs.

FOR SHORTCAKE
1 cup blanched finely ground almond flour
1 teaspoon Swerve granular
½ teaspoon baking powder
¼ teaspoon kosher salt
2 tablespoons cold butter, cubed
4 large cold egg whites

FOR BERRIES
2 cups sliced strawberries
1 teaspoon Swerve confectioners

FOR WHIPPED CREAM
¾ cup heavy cream
2 teaspoons Swerve confectioners
½ teaspoon pure vanilla extract
Pinch of kosher salt

1. Make shortcakes: Preheat oven to 400°. Line a baking sheet with parchment paper.

2. In a food processor, pulse almond flour, sweetener, baking powder, and salt until well combined. Add butter and pulse until butter is about pea size. Add egg whites and pulse until combined. Butter will be in tiny little pieces, which is okay.

3. Using an ice cream scoop or measuring cup, scoop 4 shortcakes evenly spaced on prepared baking sheet. Bake until light golden and dough bounces back when lightly pressed with a finger, about 12 to 15 minutes. Let cool on baking sheet.

4. Make berries: In a medium bowl, toss berries with sweetener. Let sit while you beat cream.

5. Make whipped cream: In a large bowl using a handheld mixer, beat heavy cream, sweetener, vanilla, and a pinch of salt until medium peaks form.

6. Slice shortcakes in half and place bottoms on 4 plates. Top each bottom with a spoonful of berries. Top berries with whipped cream. Close sandwich. Over top of shortcakes spoon remaining berries and whipped cream.

NUTRITION (per serving):

416 calories
11 g protein
17 g carbohydrates
5 g fiber
7 g sugar
37 g fat
15 g saturated fat
292 mg sodium
3 g sugar alcohol

NUTRITION (per serving):

271 calories
6 g protein
13 g carbohydrates
5 g fiber
4 g sugar
24 g fat
9 g saturated fat
101 mg sodium
3 g sugar alcohol

STRAWBERRY GALETTE

 SERVES 8   **TOTAL TIME: 3 HR 20 MIN**

If the thought of crimping pie crust or weaving lattices gives you mild anxiety, make a galette instead. Any imperfection is considered "rustic" and beautiful.

FOR CRUST
1½ cups almond flour
3 tablespoons coconut flour
1 tablespoon Swerve granular
¼ teaspoon xanthan gum
¼ teaspoon baking powder
¼ teaspoon kosher salt
½ cup (1 stick) cold butter, cubed
1 large egg, beaten
Heavy cream, for brushing

FOR FILLING
1 pound strawberries, quartered
2 teaspoons Swerve granular
Juice of ½ lemon

1. Make crust: In a food processor, pulse together almond flour, coconut flour, sweetener, xanthan gum, baking powder, and salt. Add butter and pulse until mostly pea-sized, then add egg and pulse just until incorporated. Remove from food processor and pat into a smooth flat disc and wrap in plastic wrap. Refrigerate until well chilled, at least 2 hours.

2. Make filling: Preheat oven to 375°. Combine strawberries, sweetener, and lemon juice in a medium bowl and let sit for 10 minutes, then drain strawberries.

3. While strawberries drain, roll out dough. Place chilled dough between 2 pieces of parchment paper and roll into a 10-inch circle, about ¼ inch thick. If dough cracks, pinch it back together. Place dough in freezer for 10 minutes.

4. Place dough on a large baking sheet and remove top piece of parchment paper. Pile strawberries in middle of crust leaving a 1-inch border. Use bottom piece of parchment paper to help fold crust over strawberries around edge. Brush edges with heavy cream.

5. Bake until golden, 30 minutes. Let cool 20 minutes before slicing.

BERRY CRISP

 SERVES 10   **TOTAL TIME: 40 MIN**

This recipe can be thrown together in less than an hour with minimal effort. The cinnamon pecan crumble is the perfect pairing for the lemon-kissed berries.

Cooking spray
1 (6-ounce) package raspberries
1 (6-ounce) package blackberries
1 cup hulled and sliced strawberries
1 teaspoon lemon zest
2 teaspoons lemon juice
1 teaspoon liquid stevia, divided
1 teaspoon pure vanilla extract
2 tablespoons plus ¾ cup almond flour, divided
¾ cup finely chopped pecans
2 tablespoons ground flaxseed
¼ teaspoon ground cinnamon
3 tablespoons butter, softened

1. Preheat oven to 350° and grease an 8-inch baking dish with cooking spray. In a large bowl, mix berries, lemon zest and juice, ½ teaspoon stevia, vanilla, and 2 tablespoons almond flour. Spread mixture into bottom of prepared dish.

2. In a medium bowl, add remaining ¾ cup almond flour, pecans, flaxseed, cinnamon, remaining ½ teaspoon stevia, and butter. Using a fork, toss until coarse crumbs form. Sprinkle over berries.

3. Bake until crumble is golden, about 30 to 35 minutes. Cool slightly before serving.

NUTRITION (per serving):

170 calories
4 g protein
9 g carbohydrates
5 g fiber
3 g sugar
15 g fat
3 g saturated fat
35 mg sodium
0 g sugar alcohol

NUTRITION (per serving):

428 calories
8 g protein
32 g carbohydrates
11 g fiber
4 g sugar
40 g fat
13 g saturated fat
120 mg sodium
15 g sugar alcohol

"APPLE" CRISP

SERVES 6 | **TOTAL TIME: 1 HR 30 MIN**

Sadly, apples are fairly high in carbs. What's not: zucchini. We know, we know. Replacing a Granny Smith with a summer squash doesn't feel like a fair swap. But trust us—it works.

FOR FILLING
- 2½ pounds zucchini, peeled and halved lengthwise (3 large)
- ⅓ cup brown Swerve
- 1 tablespoon butter
- 2 teaspoons fresh lemon juice
- 1½ teaspoons ground cinnamon
- 2 teaspoons pure vanilla extract
- ¼ teaspoon kosher salt

FOR CRUMBLE
- 1 cup blanched finely ground almond flour
- ¼ cup coconut flour
- 2 tablespoons brown Swerve
- Pinch of kosher salt
- 1 cup chopped toasted pecans
- 7 tablespoons butter, melted and cooled slightly, plus more for brushing

1. Make filling: Using a spoon, scrape seeds from center of each zucchini half and slice crosswise into ¼-inch-thick pieces.

2. In a large pot, combine zucchini, sweetener, butter, lemon juice, cinnamon, vanilla, and salt. Place over medium heat and cook, stirring occasionally, until zucchini releases juices and juices thicken, about 15 minutes. Remove from heat.

3. Preheat oven to 350°. In a medium bowl, whisk together almond flour, coconut flour, sweetener, and salt, breaking up any large pieces with fingers, if necessary. Add pecans and butter and stir until combined and clumps form.

4. Brush a 1-quart cast-iron pan or baking dish with butter. Scrape zucchini mixture into prepared baking dish. Scatter crumble over top. Bake until top is golden and juices are bubbling around edges, about 25 minutes. Let cool slightly before serving.

PRO TIP! Want to splurge for actual apples? Sub in 3 apples for the zucchini, reduce the brown Swerve to ¼ cup, and increase the baking time to 45 minutes.

PIES & COBBLERS | 121

CHAPTER SEVEN
ICE CREAM, ETC.

FROZEN YOGURT BITES

 SERVES 5   **TOTAL TIME: 2 HR 10 MIN**

You're going to want to keep a stash of these creamy, colorful discs in the freezer at all times. And if you're smart, you'll hide them.

1 cup full-fat Greek yogurt
½ cup blueberries
½ teaspoon pure vanilla extract

1. Line a large baking sheet with parchment paper. Combine all ingredients in blender (or a food processor) and blend until smooth.

2. Transfer mixture to a piping bag or a large resealable plastic bag and cut a small hole in corner. Pipe small dollops (about 1-inch in diameter) onto prepared baking sheet.

3. Freeze, about 2 hours. Transfer to a freezer-safe plastic bag for long-term storage.

NUTRITION (per serving):

59 calories
5 g protein
4 g carbohydrates
0 g fiber
4 g sugar
3 g fat
1 g saturated fat
18 mg sodium
0 g sugar alcohol

NUTRITION (per serving):

260 calories
5 g protein
28 g carbohydrates
4 g fiber
1 g sugar
23 g fat
12 g saturated fat
93 mg sodium
12 g sugar alcohol

FROZEN MINT CHIP PIE

 SERVES 16   **TOTAL TIME: 2 HR 20 MIN**

Ice cream cakes sound nice in theory, but in reality, if you're dealing with actual cake layers, they're difficult to assemble and even more annoying to eat. Ice cream pie is simpler and in all honesty better. (And, yes, for all intents and purposes, we're calling this filling ice cream.)

FOR CRUST
1¼ cups almond flour
¼ cup Swerve granular
3 tablespoons unsweetened cocoa powder
Kosher salt
¼ cup (½ stick) butter, melted

FOR PIE FILLING
1 cup cold heavy cream
6 ounces cream cheese, softened
1 cup Swerve confectioners
Green gel food coloring
½ teaspoon peppermint extract
Kosher salt
1¼ cups sugar-free chocolate chips, divided
2 teaspoons coconut butter

1. Make crust: In a medium bowl, mix together almond flour, sweetener, cocoa powder, salt, and melted butter. Press crumb mixture into bottom and evenly up sides of a 9-inch pie dish. Refrigerate while you make filling.

2. Make filling: Using a hand mixer or whisk, beat heavy cream until stiff peaks form. Refrigerate until ready to use.

3. In another large bowl, beat together cream cheese and sweetener until completely combined. Add food coloring, peppermint extract, and salt and beat until combined. With a rubber spatula, fold ¼ of whipped cream into cream cheese mixture until it is completely combined. Repeat three more times until all whipped cream is combined with the cream cheese mixture. Fold in more food coloring if needed.

4. Fold in 1 cup chocolate chips, then transfer mixture to prepared pie crust. Smooth top and freeze until firm, 1½ hours.

5. When ready to serve, melt remaining chocolate in microwave, stir in coconut butter, and drizzle over pie.

STRAWBERRY-LIME CHEESECAKE POPS

 MAKES 8　　 **TOTAL TIME: 5 HR 15 MIN**

We'll never give up on finding ways to sneak cheesecake into your day in a wide array of different forms. Fat bomb, brownie, popsicle… nothing is off limits.

1½ (8-ounce) blocks cream cheese, softened
1½ cups chopped strawberries
¼ cup Swerve confectioners
Zest of 1 lime
2 teaspoons fresh lime juice
¾ cup heavy cream

1. In food processor, combine cream cheese, strawberries, and sweetener and pulse until smooth. Transfer to a large bowl and stir in lime zest and juice.

2. In a separate large bowl using a hand mixer, beat heavy cream until stiff peaks form. Fold whipped cream into cream cheese mixture until incorporated.

3. Divide between popsicle molds and insert a popsicle stick into each mold. Cover and freeze until firm, 4 to 5 hours.

NUTRITION (per serving):

236 calories
3 g protein
10 g carbohydrates
1 g fiber
4 g sugar
23 g fat
14 g saturated fat
140 mg sodium
5 g sugar alcohol

ICE CREAM, ETC. | 129

NUTRITION (per serving):

97 calories
2 g protein
9 g carbohydrates
2 g fiber
0.21 g sugar
10 g fat
5 g saturated fat
133 mg sodium
6 g sugar alcohol

ICE CREAM SANDWICHES

 SERVES 12   **TOTAL TIME: 4 HR 30 MIN**

No offense to the Chipwich, but nothing compares to a classic ice cream sandwich—the kind with soft rectangular chocolate cookies on both ends.

Cooking spray
¾ cup unsweetened cocoa powder
⅔ cup almond flour
⅔ cup Swerve confectioners
1 teaspoon baking soda
¾ teaspoon kosher salt
½ cup (1 stick) butter, melted
2 large eggs
3 cups keto-friendly ice cream

1. Preheat oven to 350°. Line a large baking sheet with parchment paper and grease with cooking spray. In a large bowl, whisk together cocoa powder, almond flour, sweetener, baking soda, and salt. Add melted butter and eggs and whisk until just combined. Using an offset spatula, spread batter into an even layer on prepared baking sheet.

2. Bake until barely set and a toothpick inserted in middle comes out clean, about 7 minutes. Let cool completely.

3. Line another large baking sheet with parchment paper, then flip cooled cookie onto it. Cut in half widthwise.

4. Let ice cream sit until softened slightly, then spread over one half using an offset spatula. To help spread ice cream, run your offset under hot water and wipe off with a paper towel. Use parchment to help flip the other half on top and press to make sure it is sandwiched well. Freeze until completely solid, at least 4 hours.

5. Cut into 24 squares that are 2x2-inch each and keep in freezer until ready to serve.

FROSTY

 SERVES 4   **TOTAL TIME: 45 MIN**

Making ice cream usually involves a grueling 4 to 5 hours of waiting for the mixture to freeze properly. With this recipe, you only need 30 minutes. It's a mother-effing frosty miracle.

- 1½ cups heavy cream
- 2 tablespoons unsweetened cocoa powder
- 3 tablespoons Swerve confectioners
- 1 teaspoon pure vanilla extract
- Pinch kosher salt

1. In a large bowl, combine cream, cocoa, sweetener, vanilla, and salt. Using a hand mixer or the whisk attachment of a stand mixer, beat mixture until stiff peaks form. Scoop mixture into a Ziploc bag and freeze 30 to 35 minutes, until just frozen.

2. Cut tip off a corner of bag and pipe into glasses.

NUTRITION (per serving):

317 calories
3 g protein
11 g carbohydrates
2 g fiber
3 g sugar
33 g fat
21 g saturated fat
54 mg sodium
5 g sugar alcohol

ICE CREAM, ETC. | 133

NUTRITION (per serving):

- 323 calories
- 4 g protein
- 6 g carbohydrates
- 1 g fiber
- 2 g sugar
- 39 g fat
- 30 g saturated fat
- 45 mg sodium
- 4 g sugar alcohol

MIX IT UP!

CHOCOLATE: Melt 2 cups sugar-free chocolate chips with 2 tablespoons coconut oil. Fold into mixture in Step 4.

STRAWBERRY: Blend 2 cups chopped strawberries until it resembles a loose jam, then stir in 2 cups chopped strawberries and set aside. Fold into mixture in Step 4.

MINT CHIP: Add ½ teaspoon mint extract to whipped cream, and use food coloring to dye mixture green. Fold in chocolate chips in Step 4.

COFFEE: Stir together ¼ cup hot water and 2 tablespoons instant coffee. Fold into mixture in Step 4.

COOKIE DOUGH: Beat 1 cup softened butter with ⅔ cup Swerve confectioners, 1 teaspoon pure vanilla extract, and 1½ teaspoons kosher salt. Stir in 4 cups almond flour and 1 cup keto-friendly chocolate chips. Roll into small bite-size balls. Fold into mixture in Step 4.

COCONUT VANILLA ICE CREAM

 SERVES 8   **TOTAL TIME: 8 HR 15 MIN**

We don't just love this homemade ice cream because it's outrageously creamy. We adore it for how infinitely adaptable it is.

2 (15-ounce) cans coconut milk
2 cups heavy cream
¼ cup Swerve confectioners
1 teaspoon pure vanilla extract
Pinch of kosher salt

1. Chill coconut milk in fridge at least 3 hours, or ideally overnight.

2. Make whipped coconut: Spoon coconut cream into a large bowl, leaving liquid in can, and use a hand mixer to beat coconut cream until very creamy. Set aside.

3. Make whipped cream: In a separate large bowl using a hand mixer (or in bowl of a stand mixer), beat heavy cream until soft peaks form. Beat in sweetener, vanilla, and salt.

4. Fold whipped coconut into whipped cream, then transfer mixture into a loaf pan.

5. Freeze until solid, about 5 hours.

AVOCADO POPS

MAKES 10 | **TOTAL TIME: 6 HR 10 MIN**

At this point in the book, we're all aboard the avocados + chocolate train, right? Great. Because now we're adding coconut milk and limes to the mix. And in the words of one online recipe review, "Holy guacamole these are amazing."

- 3 ripe avocados
- Juice of 2 limes (about ⅓ cup)
- 3 tablespoons Swerve granular
- ¾ cup coconut milk
- 1 tablespoon coconut oil
- 1 cup sugar-free dark chocolate chips

1. In a blender or food processor, combine avocados with lime juice, sweetener, and coconut milk. Blend until smooth. Pour into popsicle molds and insert a popsicle stick into each mold.
2. Freeze until firm, 6 hours or up to overnight.
3. In a medium bowl, combine coconut oil and chocolate chips. Microwave until melted, then let cool to room temperature. Dunk frozen pops in chocolate and serve.

NUTRITION (per serving):

120 calories
1 g protein
5 g carbohydrates
3 g fiber
0 g sugar
12 g fat
5 g saturated fat
5 mg sodium
11 g sugar alcohol

ICE CREAM, ETC. | 137

CHAPTER EIGHT

HOLIDAY ESSENTIALS

PUMPKIN CHEESECAKE

SERVES 16 | **TOTAL TIME: 7 HR 30 MIN**

You don't need a reason to make pumpkin cheesecake. The cheesecake is your reason to celebrate. (But be careful. It's hard to stop at just one slice.)

FOR CRUST
- 1½ cups almond flour
- ¼ cup coconut flour
- 2 tablespoons Swerve granular
- ½ teaspoon cinnamon
- ¼ teaspoon kosher salt
- 7 tablespoons butter, melted

FOR FILLING
- 4 (8-ounce) blocks cream cheese, softened
- ½ cup brown Swerve
- 1 cup pumpkin puree
- 3 large eggs
- 1 teaspoon pure vanilla extract
- 1 teaspoon cinnamon
- ½ teaspoon ground ginger
- ¼ teaspoon kosher salt
- Whipped cream, for garnish
- Chopped toasted pecans, for garnish

1. Preheat oven to 350°. In a medium bowl, combine almond flour, coconut flour, sweetener, cinnamon, and salt. Add melted butter and mix until well combined. Press crust into an 8-inch springform pan in an even layer and a little up sides. Bake until lightly golden, 10 to 15 minutes.

2. Reduce oven to 325°. In a large bowl with a handheld mixer, beat cream cheese and sweetener together until light and fluffy. Add pumpkin puree and beat until no lumps remain. Add eggs, one at a time, and beat until well combined. Add vanilla, cinnamon, ginger, and salt. Pour batter on top of crust and smooth top with an offset spatula.

3. Wrap bottom of pan in aluminum foil and place in a large roasting pan. Pour in enough boiling water to come up halfway in baking pan.

4. Bake until center of cheesecake only slightly jiggles, about 1 hour. Turn off heat, prop open oven door, and let cheesecake cool in oven, 1 hour.

5. Remove foil and refrigerate cheesecake until completely chilled, at least 5 hours and up to overnight.

6. Serve with a dollop of whipped cream and toasted pecans.

NUTRITION (per serving):

377 calories
8 g protein
18 g carbohydrates
4 g fiber
4 g sugar
36 g fat
17 g saturated fat
261 mg sodium
8 g sugar alcohol

NUTRITION (per serving):

279 calories
5 g protein
23 g carbohydrates
4 g fiber
2 g sugar
27 g fat
16 g saturated fat
84 mg sodium
16 g sugar alcohol

CHRISTMAS EGGNOG

 SERVES 6   **TOTAL TIME: 1 HR 35 MIN**

Never underestimate the power of a good eggnog during the holiday season. When paired with a great movie and some sparkly lights (and maybe a teeny tiny splash of rum), homemade eggnog can lift your spirits like no other.

FOR EGGNOG
6 large egg yolks
½ cup Swerve granular
1 cup heavy cream
1 teaspoon pure vanilla extract
Large pinch of freshly grated nutmeg, plus more for topping
Pinch of ground cinnamon
2 cups unsweetened almond milk

FOR TOPPING
½ cup heavy cream
6 cinnamon sticks, for serving

1. In a medium bowl, whisk together egg yolks and sweetener until light and fluffy.

2. In a small saucepan, heat heavy cream over medium heat, stirring frequently, until it comes to a simmer. While whisking, slowly and carefully pour heated heavy cream into egg mixture. When fully combined, scrape mixture back into saucepan and return to medium heat. Cook, stirring constantly, until mixture is thick enough to coat back of a spoon, about 3 to 5 minutes.

3. Remove from heat and strain through a fine-mesh sieve into a heatproof bowl. Add vanilla, nutmeg, and cinnamon and stir to combine. Let cool slightly, then cover surface of heavy cream mixture with plastic (to prevent a film from forming) and refrigerate until well chilled, at least 1 hour.

4. When ready to serve, make topping: In a medium bowl, whisk heavy cream just until firm peaks form. Set aside.

5. Remove plastic from chilled heavy cream mixture and whisk until smooth (it should be pudding-like in consistency). Add almond milk and whisk into chilled heavy cream mixture until smooth. Pour eggnog into glasses and dollop with whipped cream. Grate fresh nutmeg over top and add a cinnamon stick.

GINGERBREAD COOKIES

MAKES 18 | **TOTAL TIME: 4 HR**

Cinnamon, ginger, cloves, and nutmeg are what make gingerbread taste so nostalgic and Christmas-y. Not carbs.

FOR COOKIES
- 2½ cups blanched finely ground almond flour, plus more for dusting
- ¼ cup finely ground coconut flour
- 1 tablespoon ground ginger
- 1 tablespoon ground cinnamon
- ¾ teaspoon ground cloves
- ½ teaspoon freshly grated nutmeg
- ½ teaspoon baking soda
- ¼ teaspoon kosher salt
- ¾ cup (1½ sticks) butter, softened
- ⅓ cup Swerve granular

FOR ROYAL ICING
- 1 cup Swerve confectioners
- 2 tablespoons meringue powder
- 1 tablespoon fresh lemon juice
- ¼ cup water

1. Make cookies: In a large bowl, whisk together almond flour, coconut flour, ginger, cinnamon, cloves, nutmeg, baking soda, and salt. In another large bowl, beat butter and sweetener until light and fluffy, about 2 minutes. Add dry ingredients to butter mixture and beat to combine.

2. Wrap dough in plastic and refrigerate for at least 1 hour or up to overnight.

3. Preheat oven to 350°. Line two baking sheets with parchment paper.

4. Roll out dough between two sheets of parchment paper. Dust dough on both sides with almond flour if dough is too sticky. Freeze until firm (while still between parchment paper) for about 30 minutes.

5. Loosen paper from one side, flip, and remove paper from top of dough. Cut cookies as desired and use a thin metal spatula to transfer cookies to prepared baking sheets. Scraps can be rerolled and refrozen before cutting.

6. Freeze cutout cookies for 15 minutes. Bake cookies for 10 to 12 minutes until crisp and just starting to turn golden on edges. Cool completely on trays on a wire rack. Use a thin metal spatula to loosen cookies.

7. Make royal icing: In a stand mixer fitted with the whisk attachment, whisk all ingredients on high speed until thick and white, about 7 minutes. Thin with water or add more sweetener to achieve desired consistency, if necessary. Put into piping bags or bottles to decorate. Let icing dry at least 1 hour.

NUTRITION (per serving):

177 calories
4 g protein
18 g carbohydrates
3 g fiber
1 g sugar
16 g fat
6 g saturated fat
75 mg sodium
12 g sugar alcohol

HOLIDAY ESSENTIALS | 145

NUTRITION (per serving):

234 calories
4 g protein
20 g carbohydrates
6 g fiber
2 g sugar
23 g fat
15 g saturated fat
19 mg sodium
10 g sugar alcohol

HOT CHOCOLATE

SERVES 1 | **TOTAL TIME: 10 MIN**

Making your hot cocoa with heavy cream instead of milk doesn't just make it keto-friendly, it makes it so 👏 much 👏 better 👏.

- 2 tablespoons unsweetened cocoa powder, plus more for garnish
- 2½ teaspoons Swerve granular
- 1¼ cups water, divided
- ¼ cup heavy cream
- ¼ teaspoon pure vanilla extract
- Whipped cream, for serving

1. In a small saucepan over medium-low heat, whisk together cocoa, sweetener, and about 2 tablespoons water until smooth and dissolved. Increase heat to medium, add remaining water and cream and whisk occasionally until hot.

2. Stir in vanilla then pour into a mug. Serve with whipped cream and a dusting of cocoa powder.

HOLIDAY ESSENTIALS | 147

ALMOND CRUNCH TOFFEE

SERVES 8-10   **TOTAL TIME: 2 HR**

According to Laura, one of our trusty recipe developers who worked on 20+ recipes in this book, this sweet and salty snack was her absolute favorite.

FOR ALMOND CRUNCH
- 2 cups blanched finely ground almond flour, plus more for dusting
- ¼ cup Swerve confectioners
- ½ teaspoon baking powder
- ¼ teaspoon ground cinnamon
- 1 large egg, beaten
- 2 tablespoons butter, melted

FOR TOFFEE TOPPING
- ½ cup (1 stick) butter
- ¼ cup packed brown Swerve

FOR CHOCOLATE TOPPING
- ¾ cup sugar-free dark chocolate chips
- 1 tablespoon coconut oil
- ½ cup finely chopped pecans

1. Make almond crunch: Preheat oven to 325°. In a medium bowl, whisk together almond flour, sweetener, baking powder, and cinnamon. Add egg and butter and stir well to fully combine. It will be a thicker dough (like pie dough).

2. Form almond mixture into a ball and place on a sheet of parchment paper. Using a rolling pin, roll out dough to a scant ¼-inch-thick circle, and dust top lightly with more almond flour if dough is sticking to rolling pin. Slide parchment with dough on it onto a baking sheet and bake until golden, about 22 to 25 minutes. Let cool on a wire rack, about 20 minutes.

3. Make toffee topping: In a small saucepan over medium heat, melt butter and sweetener, stirring. Bring to a boil and cook, stirring, until amber in color (about a shade or two darker than its original color—essentially, butter browns a bit), about 2 to 3 minutes. Immediately remove pan from heat and carefully pour on top of baked almond crunch. Use a spoon to spread to edges, leaving a ¼- to ⅛-inch border. Let cool until hardened, about 30 minutes.

4. Make chocolate topping: In a medium microwave-safe bowl, combine chocolate chips and coconut oil. Microwave until just melted, stirring a few times, about 1 minute. Pour chocolate on top of toffee topping and spread in an even layer. Sprinkle with pecans.

5. Refrigerate until chocolate is firm, about 20 minutes. Break into pieces.

NUTRITION (per serving):

415 calories
8 g protein
27 g carbohydrates
10 g fiber
2 g sugar
39 g fat
14 g saturated fat
45 mg sodium
9 g sugar alcohol

NUTRITION (per serving):

351 calories
10 g protein
23 g carbohydrates
8 g fiber
4 g sugar
31 g fat
13 g saturated fat
194 mg sodium
12 g sugar alcohol

PUMPKIN PIE

 SERVES 8   **TOTAL TIME: 3 HR**

Pumpkin pie isn't just a Thanksgiving staple—it's a necessary part of the holiday. And no offense to your lovely Aunt Deborah's recipe, but no one will miss it when this is on the table.

FOR CRUST
1½ cups almond flour
3 tablespoons coconut flour
¼ teaspoon baking powder
¼ teaspoon kosher salt
4 tablespoons butter, melted
1 large egg, beaten

FOR FILLING
1 (15-ounce) can pumpkin puree
1 cup heavy cream
½ cup packed brown Swerve
3 large eggs, beaten
1 teaspoon ground cinnamon
½ teaspoon ground ginger
¼ teaspoon ground nutmeg
¼ teaspoon ground cloves
¼ teaspoon kosher salt
1 teaspoon pure vanilla extract
Whipped cream, for serving (optional)

1. Make crust: Preheat oven to 350°. In a large bowl, whisk together almond flour, coconut flour, baking powder, and salt. Add melted butter and egg and stir until a dough forms. Press dough evenly into a 9-inch pie plate, then use a fork to poke holes all over crust.

2. Bake until lightly golden, 10 minutes.

3. Make filling: In a large bowl, whisk together pumpkin, cream, sweetener, eggs, spices, salt, and vanilla until smooth. Pour pumpkin mixture into par-baked crust.

4. Bake until filling is slightly jiggly in middle and crust is golden, 45 to 50 minutes.

5. Turn off oven and prop door open. Let pie cool in oven for 1 hour, then refrigerate until ready to serve.

6. Serve with whipped cream, if desired.

BEST-EVER FUDGE

 MAKES 36   **TOTAL TIME: 30 MIN**

Fudge never gets enough credit around the holidays. Everyone is fixated on the dang cookies. We love cookies, please don't get us wrong, but come December, we're already a little tired of baking. Fudge is simpler, chocolatey-er, and just as festive.

Cooking spray
1 (8-ounce) block cream cheese, softened
4 tablespoons (½ stick) butter, softened
1 cup Swerve confectioners
1 cup unsweetened cocoa powder
½ cup heavy cream
1½ cups sugar-free dark chocolate chips, melted
½ cup finely chopped pecans

1. Grease an 8x8-inch baking pan with cooking spray. Line with parchment paper, leaving a 2-inch overhang on at least two sides. Do not grease parchment.

2. In a large bowl using a hand mixer, beat cream cheese and butter until light and fluffy. Add sweetener, cocoa powder, and heavy cream and beat until well combined.

3. In a medium microwave-safe bowl, microwave chocolate chips until just melted, about 1 minute. Add melted chocolate chips to fudge mixture and beat until combined.

4. Scrape fudge mixture into prepared baking pan. Smooth top with a spatula into an even layer. Sprinkle with pecans and gently press top, just to make sure pecans adhere but not to fully submerge them.

5. Freeze until set, 20 minutes. Slice into squares and serve. Keep any extra fudge refrigerated.

NUTRITION (per serving):

101 calories
2 g protein
11 g carbohydrates
4 g fiber
1 g sugar
9 g fat
5 g saturated fat
21 mg sodium
4 g sugar alcohol

HOLIDAY ESSENTIALS | 153

NUTRITION (per serving):

560 calories
12 g protein
28 g carbohydrates
10 g fiber
3 g sugar
54 g fat
15 g saturated fat
213 mg sodium
14 g sugar alcohol

PECAN PIE

 SERVES 8   **TOTAL TIME: 1 HR**

This pecan pie has two major things going for it. It's made without corn syrup (which in our opinion, makes pecan pie way too sweet) and made with cream. Will it be the first thing to disappear from your Thanksgiving dessert spread? Absolutely.

FOR CRUST
1½ cups blanched finely ground almond flour
3 tablespoons coconut flour
¼ teaspoon baking powder
¼ teaspoon kosher salt
4 tablespoons butter, melted
1 large egg, beaten

FOR FILLING
5 tablespoons butter
½ cup packed brown Swerve
¼ cup heavy cream
1 tablespoon pure vanilla extract
¼ teaspoon kosher salt
3 large eggs
2 cups pecan halves
1 large egg, beaten

1. Preheat oven to 350°. In a large bowl, whisk together almond flour, coconut flour, baking powder, and salt. Add melted butter and egg and stir until a dough forms. Press dough evenly into a 9-inch pie plate, then use a fork to poke holes all over crust. Bake until lightly golden, 10 to 15 minutes. Let cool 10 minutes on a wire rack.

2. In a medium saucepan over medium heat, combine butter, brown sugar, and heavy cream, stirring until mixture begins to simmer. Remove from heat and pour butter mixture into a heatproof bowl. Whisk in eggs, vanilla, and salt. Stir in pecans.

3. Bake until puffed and set in center, tenting with foil if crust darkens too fast, about 30 minutes. Let cool completely before slicing.

CHOCOLATE MOUSSE

 SERVES 4   **TOTAL TIME: 1 HR**

The end of a fancy holiday dinner calls for an equally classy dessert. Mousse might seem a little old school, but a quick glance at the ingredient list here will assure you that this is not your grandma's version.

- 2 ripe avocados
- ¾ cup heavy cream
- ½ cup sugar-free dark chocolate chips
- ¼ cup Swerve confectioners
- 3 tablespoons unsweetened cocoa powder
- 1 teaspoon pure vanilla extract
- ½ teaspoon kosher salt

1. In a food processor or blender, blend all ingredients until smooth.

2. Transfer to serving glasses and refrigerate 30 minutes and up to 1 hour.

PRO TIP! Garnish with some (sugar-free) chocolate curls if you're feelin' fancy.

156 | KETO FOR DESSERT LOVERS

NUTRITION (per serving):

446 calories
6 g protein
37 g carbohydrates
16 g fiber
3 g sugar
41 g fat
18 g saturated fat
260 mg sodium
9 g sugar alcohol

NUTRITION (per serving):

291 calories
11 g protein
25 g carbohydrates
10 g fiber
3 g sugar
23 g fat
5 g saturated fat
314 mg sodium
6 g sugar alcohol

PUMPKIN BREAD

 SERVES 8   **TOTAL TIME: 2 HR 15 MIN**

From the months of September to November, we eat this bread like it's our job. Then December rolls around and we are, once again, sick of pumpkin. By February, we're counting down the days until September, and the cycle starts anew.

Cooking spray
2 cups blanched finely ground almond flour
¼ cup Swerve granular
1½ teaspoons baking powder
¾ teaspoon baking soda
1½ teaspoons pumpkin pie spice
½ teaspoon ground cinnamon
¼ teaspoon kosher salt
1 cup pumpkin puree
3 large eggs
½ cup sugar-free dark chocolate chips
3 tablespoons raw pumpkin seeds (pepitas)

1. Preheat oven to 350°. Grease a 4x8-inch loaf pan with cooking spray and line with parchment paper, leaving a 2-inch overhang on long sides. Grease parchment.

2. In a large bowl, whisk together almond flour, sweetener, baking powder, baking soda, pumpkin pie spice, cinnamon, and salt.

3. In a medium bowl, whisk together pumpkin puree and eggs. Add wet ingredients to dry ingredients and stir to combine. Stir in chocolate chips.

4. Scrape batter into prepared loaf pan. Using a spatula, smooth top into an even layer. Sprinkle evenly with pumpkin seeds. Bake until puffed and a toothpick inserted into center comes out clean, about 50 minutes to 1 hour. If browning too fast, tent with foil after 30 minutes.

MORE FROM DELISH

You'll find everything you could possibly want in one of our cookbooks—whether it's a weeknight chicken dinner, an easy Instant Pot side, an epic air fryer appetizer, or an over-the-top dessert. **We've got it all.**

KETO FOR CARB LOVERS
100+ Amazing Low Carb, High Fat Recipes

PARTY IN AN AIR FRYER
75+ Guilt-Free Air Fryer Recipes

PARTY IN AN INSTANT POT®
75+ Crazy Simple Recipes Made in Your Multi Cooker

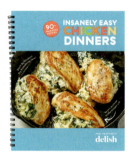

INSANELY EASY CHICKEN DINNERS
90+ Delicious Weeknight Dinners

INSANE SWEETS
100+ Cookies, Bars, Bites & Treats

ULTIMATE COCKTAILS
100+ Fun & Delicious Cocktail Recipes

EAT LIKE EVERY DAY'S THE WEEKEND
275+ Amazing Recipe Ideas!

KETO STARTER GUIDE
Essential Recipes, Tips & Tricks For Keto Beginners

INSANELY EASY CASSEROLES
80+ Easy & Comforting Casseroles

CHECK THEM OUT AT:
Store.Delish.com and Amazon